The Open Space of Democracy

by
Terry Tempest Williams

a publication of The Orion Society

The Open Space of Democracy
by Terry Tempest Williams

ISBN 0-913098-63-9
Copyright © 2004 by The Orion Society

The Orion Society
187 Main Street, Great Barrington, MA 01230
telephone: 413/528-4422   facsimile: 413/528-0676
email: orion@orionsociety.org   website: www.oriononline.org

Cover image: Detail of *Glimpse*, 1994-1995, by Mary Frank.
Courtesy of D.C. Moore Gallery, New York, NY

Designed by Jason Houston

These essays were originally serialized in *Orion* magazine.

Printed in the U.S.A. by Excelsior Printing Co.

2nd printing

Dedicated to my teachers

Florence Krall Shephard

Ted Major

J. D. Williams

and

Professor Wangari Maathai

*What threatens us today is fear....Our danger is the forces in
the world today which are trying to use man's fear to rob him of
his individuality, his soul, trying to reduce him to an unthinking
mass by fear....This is what we must resist, if we are to change
the world for man's peace and security....So never be afraid.*

*Never be afraid to raise your voice for honesty and truth and
compassion, against injustice and lying and greed. If you...will
do this, not as a class or classes, but as individuals, men and
women, you will change the earth.*

—WILLIAM FAULKNER
Address to Graduating Class, University High
School, Oxford, Mississippi, May 28, 1951

*The most painful thing to bear is seeing a mockery made of
what one loves.*

—ALBERT CAMUS

*It is possible that the next Buddha will not take the form of
an individual. The next Buddha may take the form of a community—a community practicing understanding and loving
kindness, a community practicing mindful living. This may be the
most important thing we can do for the survival of the Earth.*

—THICH NHAT HANH

The Open Space of Democracy

Foreword

Events of the past few years have not been kind to America. From the collective grief we shared witnessing the collapse of the World Trade Center to the polarized sentiments of our fellow citizens surrounding the current conflict in Iraq, we Americans have faced a tumultuous and historic time.

Now, on the eve of a defining national election, we are asking ourselves what is the true nature of democracy and the qualities of leadership necessary to guide and shape our nation and its future role in global affairs. Never has the participation of the individual citizen mattered more. Never has "the majesty of the vote" been more crucial in registering our dreams and desires.

For a democracy to be truly alive, vital, and revolutionary, for it to rise beyond abstraction and mere symbolism, for it to become a throbbing head-and-heart-felt presence in our lives, we need to make it personal.

In this fourth volume of The Orion Society's New Patriotism Series, Terry Tempest Williams has made democracy personal. She has reminded us through the power and integrity of these thoughtful essays that democracy is not simply an idea but a place—the *land* of the free. Our responsibilities to the land, like the responsibilities of freedom, are patriotism's touchstones. Rare. Sacred. Precious. And they demand our highest attention.

Williams writes, "In the open space of democracy, we are listening—ears alert—we are watching—eyes open— registering the patterns and possibilities for engagement. Some acts are private; some are public. Our oscillations between local, national, and global gestures map the full range of our movement. Our strength lies in our imagination, and paying attention to what sustains life, rather than what destroys it."

There is an essential artfulness, suppleness, and fierce advocacy at the core of such a stance on living. One is simultaneously a citizen of a place—Castle Valley, UT—a citizen of a nation and its many places—including the Arctic Refuge—and a citizen of the world. The realization that these forms of citizenship are fundamentally connected, and need to become tripartite facets of our identity, seems to me to be a principal challenge for those living in the twenty-first century.

Too often in the last few years it has been suggested that Americans need to "go it alone" in the world, and that a very limited sense of national interest define both our domestic priorities as well as our approach to foreign relations. A deteriorating environment and an unjustified, preemptive war on Iraq are just two tragic products of this line of thinking.

We need new leadership and a new process by which to engage with each other, our communities, and the rest of the world—human and more-than-human. We need a new commencement, a new gathering place. We need to ground-truth old truths. We need to spread democracy, especially in our own hearts and lives. We need to inhabit change more compassionately. And we need to heed the sage advice of those who, like Emerson, Whitman, and Carson, hold a close correspondence with the American oversoul.

Follow the words of Terry Tempest Williams and you will find yourself in the company of as important a thinker as we have in these times of terror and timorousness in our national life. A writer of brave imagination, Williams has created an authentic space of dialogue. It is our hope that her call for a "reflective activism" on behalf of a dynamic democracy will take root within our hearts as well as our public policies.

—Laurie Lane-Zucker
Executive Director & Series Editor

The Open Space
of Democracy

Meeting

COMMENCEMENT

A FIGURE DRAWN IN BLUE is arching over a deep chasm to make contact with a smaller figure outlined in black, also stretching across the divide to meet the other. The two gestures create a bridge. The artist Mary Frank has created an image of democracy. She has titled her painting: *Meeting.* The gorge that separates the two figures reminds me of a place in the Grand Canyon where Vishnu schist appears serpentine along the Colorado River that has cut waves through this stone for eons. But Frank's river is not red or white with rapids or blue, but black like oil, like greed, like grief, and suddenly, the evocative scene translates to the place we find ourselves now.

Since September 11, 2001, we have witnessed an escalation of rhetoric within the United States that has led us to war twice in two years. We have heard our president, our vice-president, our secretary of defense, and our attorney general cultivate fear and command with lies, suggesting our homeland security and safety must reside in their hands, not ours. Force has trumped debate and diplomacy.

Our language has been taken hostage. Words like patriotism, freedom, and democracy have been bound and gagged, forced to perform indecent acts through the abuse of slogans. *Freedom will prevail. We are liberating Iraq. God bless America.*

For many of us, the war on terror is not something that has been initiated outside our country, but inside our country as well. We wonder who to trust and what to believe.

I have always believed democracy is best practiced through its construction, not its completion—a never-ending project where the windows and doors remain open, a reminder to never close ourselves off to the sensory impulses of eyes and ears alert toward justice. Walls are torn down instead of erected in a counter-intuitive process where a monument is not built but a home, in a constant state of renovation.

It was within this context of witnessing America at war and contemplating democracy that I accepted an invitation to deliver the commencement address to graduating seniors at the University of Utah on May 2, 2003. I was to receive an honorary doctorate degree in the humanities. Nothing could have meant more to me than to be recognized by my own school in my own town. They know who I am and who I am not. We share a history and history is always complicated. For me, personally, the stakes couldn't have been higher.

My niece, Callie Tempest Jones, was among those graduating. She is like a daughter to my husband Brooke and me. We had other young friends who were graduating. This was a rare opportunity to openly address a new generation alongside family and friends with deep ties to this institute of higher learning. Unlike most places, where I could simply speak and leave, here I would have to speak and stay, continue living and working within my own state of Utah. I wanted to address my community honestly at this moment in time when a war was dividing so many of us.

Before the speech, I had had the great pleasure of meeting with a group of graduating seniors. When I asked them what they felt we were most in need of as a society and nation, the answer was a unified one: building community. Words like compassion and service were used, and phrases like "wanting to give something back," or "having a desire and responsibility to contribute," "to make a difference," "to come together," "to remain open and listen to opposing points of view" were all part of the discussion.

What I heard were mature voices, steady minds, speaking from a generation that had witnessed the beginning of two wars, Afghanistan and Iraq, while students at the university. They were not interested in ideas or language that polarized people: Christianity vs. Islam; Republicans vs. Democrats; Mormons vs. non-Mormons; wilderness vs. development. They talked about alternatives, solutions, how to speak a language that opens hearts rather than closes them. These students were acutely aware of complexities and hesitant to take sides before considering all the evidence.

I had fifteen minutes to speak from my heart to these young people on their graduation day. My heart was pounding.

President Machen, Senator Bennett, members of the Utah State Board of Regents, distinguished guests, faculty, family, and most especially, University of Utah graduates, it is a great privilege to stand before you this morning…

Lives change at this university. Mine did. I remember the moment. The class was American Romanticism. The professor was Dr. William Mulder. He introduced us to Ralph Waldo Emerson, Henry David Thoreau, and Emily Dickinson. It was in this course, I realized, "Yes, I am a Mormon, but I am really a Transcendentalist."

> *Hope is the thing with feathers*
> *That perches in the soul* [1]
>
> —Emily Dickinson

These words became sacred text.

I realized that in American Letters we celebrate both language and landscape, that these words, stories, and poems can create an ethical stance toward life: Melville's Great Whale; Whitman's *Leaves of Grass*; Thoreau's Walden Pond; Emerson's "Oversoul"—the natural world infused with divinity. I came to understand through an education in the humanities that knowledge is another form of democracy, the freedom of expression that leads to empathy.

It begins with our questions…

Many of you graduating today are wondering how best to serve society and make a difference in the world. You have a deep desire to find meaningful work. Many of you don't know what you want to do next.

I offer you these words from my mentor in conservation, Mardy Murie, who grew up on the Alaskan frontier and became one of the great advocates for the Arctic National Wildlife Refuge. On my graduation from college, she sent me a letter, "Don't worry about what you will do next. If you take one step with all the knowledge you have, there is usually just enough light shining to show you the next step."

I believed her.

Up until now, the words of my speech had been safe, supportive, no feathers ruffled, but I was holding questions I wanted to ask and explore.

How do we engage in conversation at a time when the definition of what it means to be a patriot is being narrowly construed? *You are either with us or against us.* Discussion is waged in absolutes not ambiguities. Corporations have more access to power than people. *We, the people.* Fear has replaced discussion. Business practices have taken precedence over public process. It doesn't matter what the United Nations advises or what world opinion may be. America in the early years of the twenty-first century has become a force unto itself. The laws it chooses to abide by are its own. What role does this leave us as individuals within a republic?

Abraham Lincoln warns: "What constitutes the

bulwark of our own liberty and independence? It is not our crowning battlements, our bristling sea coasts, our army and our navy. These are not our reliance against tyranny. All of these may be turned against us without making us weaker for the struggle. Our reliance is in the spirit which prized liberty as the heritage of all men, in all lands everywhere. Destroy this spirit and you have planted the seeds of despotism at your own doors. Familiarize yourselves with the chains of bondage and you prepare your own limbs to wear them. Accustom to trample on the rights of others and you have lost the genius of your own independence and become the fit subjects of the first cunning tyrant who rises among you."[2]

I knew where my father was sitting, how uncomfortable he must have been, given his conservative point of view, complicated by his feelings for me. I knew Brooke's father was somewhere in this audience of 15,000 individuals, comprised of so many of the people I grew up with who had children of their own graduating. I wondered what my brother Steve and his wife, Ann, were thinking. This was to be a day of celebration not criticism.

How do we engage in responsive citizenship in times of terror? Do we have the imagination to rediscover an authentic patriotism that inspires empathy and reflection over pride and nationalism?

I would submit that we can protect and preserve the open space of democracy by carrying a healthy sense of indignation within us that will shatter the complacency that has seeped into our society in the name of all we have lost—knowing there is still so much to be saved.

What does the open space of democracy look like?

In the open space of democracy there is room for dissent.

In the open space of democracy there is room for differences.

In the open space of democracy, the health of the environment is seen as the wealth of our communities. We remember that our character has been shaped by the diversity of America's landscapes and it is precisely that character that will protect it. Cooperation is valued more than competition; prosperity becomes the caretaker of poverty. The humanities are not peripheral, but the very art of what it means to be human.

In the open space of democracy, beauty is not optional, but essential to our survival as a species. And technology is not rendered at the expense of life, but developed out of a reverence for life.

Reverence for life.

I was halfway through the speech with my heart still pounding. It was difficult to establish eye contact with anyone but those students and faculty in the front rows. I recognized a bright young man graduating in English who I had spoken with the week before about his future plans. He was heading to Harvard with a passion for Milton. He gave me courage.

> In the future, brave men and women will write a Declaration of Interdependence that will be read and honored alongside the Declaration of Independence: proof of our evolution, revolution of our own growth and understanding.
>
> The open space of democracy provides justice for all living things—plants, animals, rocks, and rivers, as well as human beings. It is a landscape that encourages diversity and discourages conformity.
>
> Democracy can also be messy and chaotic. It requires patience and persistence.
>
> In the open space of democracy, every vote counts and every vote is counted.

I could feel the Republicans in the Huntsman Center (thousands of them) thinking, "Here's just another two-bit liberal grousing over the fact that George W. Bush is in the White House instead of Al Gore. Get over it."

Stay focused, I said to myself, follow the words.

> When minds close, democracy begins to close. Fear creeps in; silence overtakes speech. Rhetoric masquer-

ades as thought. Dogma is dressed up like an idea. And we are told what to do, not asked what we think. Security is guaranteed. The lie begins to carry more power than the truth until the words of our own founding fathers are forgotten and the images of television replace history.

An open democracy inspires wisdom and the dignity of choice. A closed society inspires terror and the tyranny of belief. We are no longer citizens. We are media-engineered clones wondering who we are and why we feel alone. Lethargy trumps participation. We fall prey to the cynicism of our own resignation.

When democracy disappears, we are asked to accept the way things are.

I beg you, as graduates of this distinguished university, do not accept the way things are.

I finally relax and find my footing. This is for Callie, this is for all of these beautiful, free-thinking, hope-filled graduates, not yet cynical, who will carry their idealism forward.

Question. Stand. Speak. Act.

Patriots act—they are not handed a piece of paper called by that same name and asked to comply.

To engage in responsive citizenship, we must become citizens who respond. Passionately. This is how we can make a difference. This is how we can serve society.

What is at stake? Everything we value, cherish, and love. Democracy.

It was true in 1776. And it is true in 2003. This is the commitment we make to a living, breathing, evolving republic.

Thomas Jefferson said, "I believe in perilous liberty over quiet servitude."[3]

May we commit ourselves to "perilous liberty."

This is the path of intellectual freedom and spiritual curiosity. Our insistence on democracy is based on our resistance to complacency. To be engaged. To participate. To create alternatives together. We may be wrong. We will make mistakes. But we can engage in spirited conversation and listen to one another with respect and open minds as we speak and explore our differences, cherishing the vitality of the struggle.

Democracy is built upon the right to be insecure. We are vulnerable. And we are vulnerable together.

Democracy is a beautiful experiment.

Thoreau wrote in his essay, "Civil Disobedience," "Cast your whole vote, not a strip of paper merely, but your whole influence."[4]

I want to tell you a story:

On March 8, thousands of women and children gathered in Washington, D.C., for a Code Pink rally in the name of peace. We walked from Martin Luther King Park through the streets of the nation's capital to

Lafayette Park, located directly in front of the White House. When we arrived we were met by a wall of Washington, D.C. police outfitted with black combat gear, bulletproof vests, and rifles. We were not allowed to proceed on to the public park.

Medea Benjamin, one of the organizers of Code Pink, began to negotiate with the police. While these negotiations were underway, Rachel Bagby, an African-American poet and musician, stood directly across from a policeman and focused her attention on one officer in particular, also African American. She began singing with all the power of her God-given voice, "All we are saying is give peace a chance." Over and over she kept singing, "All we are saying is give peace a chance." Other women began to join her. She never took her eyes off that man, but just kept singing to him in her low, dignified voice. In that moment, it was clear neither one of them would be who they are, or where they are, without the voices of dissent uttered by their parents, without the literal acts of civil disobedience practiced by their parents' parents and their parents' parents before them.

The African-American policeman quietly stepped aside creating the opening we walked through.[5]

This is what the open space of democracy looks like.

Question. Stand. Speak. Act.
Make us uncomfortable.
Make us think.

Make us feel.
Keep us free.

—

The commencement address was met with both boos and applause in equal parts, as far as I could tell. Many students in the College of Business sat in their seats defiantly, breaking their code of good behavior by cupping their hands around their mouths yelling in the negative. Utah Senator Bob Bennett and former Senator Jake Garn had their heads bowed in disapproval. Students in the College of Humanities were on their feet cheering with much of the faculty. It did not feel personal. I simply witnessed my hometown mirror the ideological split alive in our nation.

Other writers who spoke at graduation ceremonies in May of 2003 were also met with a similar response. Chris Hedges, author of *War Is a Force that Gives Us Meaning*, questioned George W. Bush's rationale for waging war in Iraq and was unable to finish his speech at Rockford College in northern Illinois, due to heckling students, many whom stormed the stage and cut power to the microphone. He was escorted offsite by campus security.

Paul Loeb, author of *Soul of a Citizen*, was booed for criticizing President Bush and his foreign policy while giving the commencement address at Plymouth State College in New Hampshire.

But the disturbances during commencement addresses around the country were not just carried out by conservative students. At Smith College, former Secretary of State Madeleine Albright was heckled seven minutes into her talk, until she promised to meet with the protestors after her speech. While she was speaking of the extraordinary courage exhibited by those on Flight 93 over Pennsylvania, one man in the audience ran on stage carrying a banner that read, "This is why they hate us."

The spring of 2003 was a moment in time of unseemly American bravado. We had arrived in Baghdad with unprecedented speed and relatively little opposition, as a long convoy of humvees and tanks rolled into the ancient city. We watched the statue of Saddam Hussein crash to the ground with Iraqis beating his fallen body with the soles of their shoes. American casualties were few and a kick-ass attitude more akin to football than war permeated this country like a fever.

On May 1, George W. Bush had arrived on the U.S.S. *Abraham Lincoln* as a Tom Cruise look-alike, complete in his flight suit, and proclaimed his version of victory and the end of major military combat. Above our president's head waved a banner: MISSION ACCOMPLISHED. For some Americans, this was a star-spangled moment, for others, the banner read as a perverse kind of subtitle to a bad movie. Those of us who protested the war, and there were millions around the world who joined us, were told to eat crow.

After the graduation ceremony, Tom Korologos, another recipient of an honorary degree (a Utah native and powerful lobbyist in Washington, D.C., who after being named a senior advisor to Paul Bremer successfully persuaded Congress to release $87 billion for the ongoing war in Iraq), extended his hand and with wry humor quietly said, "You don't know what the hell you are talking about. I'd like to take you to Baghdad and see what you'd say then." As we walked off the stage together, he was waving a small American flag.[6]

Afterwards, Senator Bennett, our neighbor and former Mormon bishop, took me aside and in a brief conversation said, "In the spirit of democracy, I want to register my strong dissent to your talk." We shook hands and looked directly into one another's eyes. "You've inspired me to write you a letter," he said.

A few weeks later, I received a four-page, single-spaced letter from Senator Bennett dated May 7, 2003. It was not on official stationery, but plain paper straight out of his own computer.

Dear Terry:

....As I listened to you outline things that are important to you, an interesting question popped into my mind: What would she be willing to die for? Waging war always creates the risk of dying, so any discussion of war raises that issue. Then I asked myself what I would be willing to die for. The answers that came were predictable, at the front

end—family, certainly—followed by church, protection of community, and yes, finally, the cause of freedom, for others as well as my own family and friends.

That is what went on in Iraq. To use Colin Powell's comment, which I quoted to you, America has sent brave young men and women voluntarily all across the world to fight for peace and freedom. We did it this time not only for Americans but for Iraqis and all the others in the Middle East who will benefit enormously as a result of the removal of Saddam Hussein. "Greater love hath no man than this," Jesus said, than that he "will lay down his life for his friends." I think the willingness to risk death in the cause of freedom for others deserves enormous respect. Again, as Powell said, we do not do it for territory…"

I put down the letter. He had asked a provocative question. What was I willing to die for? Like Senator Bennett, I come from a religious tradition where the founder, Joseph Smith, was murdered for his religious convictions. There is no shortage of martyrs among Mormons. I also recognized the long line of military service in my family. We grew up on war stories told to us by our great uncles who served in World War II and my cousin, Scott Dixon, has never fully recovered from the horrors he witnessed in the first Gulf War, where he was a translator for generals, having learned Arabic shortly after serving his mission for the LDS Church.

It occurred to me, over the many weeks that it took me to respond to Senator Bennett's letter, that what mattered most to me was not what I was willing to die for, but what I was willing to give my life to. In war, death by belief is centered on principles both activated and extinguished in the drama of a random moment. Heroes are buried. A legacy of freedom is maintained through pain. Life by belief is centered on the day-to-day decisions we make that are largely unseen. One produces martyrs born out of violence. The other produces quiet citizens born out of personal commitments toward social change. Both dwell in the hallowed ground of sacrifice.

—

Recently, my niece Sara and I visited the Chicago Institute of Art. She had just finished a class in art history. We stood before George Seurat's painting *Sunday Afternoon in the Park.* "What the Impressionists knew," Sara said, "was that if they placed primary colors side by side through the technique of pointillism, the eye would blend the colors together."

Her comment made me think of how we might face the polarity of opinion in our country right now, how we might take opposing views and blend them into some kind of civil dialogue. This is not easy. Since George W. Bush took the office of President of the United States I have been sick at heart, unable to stomach or abide by this administration's aggressive policies directed against the environment, education, social services, healthcare, and our civil liberties—basically, the wholesale destruction of seemingly everything that contributes to a free society, except the special interests of big business.

In my darkest moments, I rant and write polemics as I watch a war of exploitation being waged against our public lands in the American West and Alaska, be it the press of coal-bed methane gas in the Powder Basin of Wyoming at the expense of precious water; the removal of wilderness protection in Utah, which translates to 200 million acres of public lands now open for business in a deal struck behind closed doors between Secretary of the Interior Gale Norton and Utah Governor Michael Leavitt, now head of the Environmental Protection Agency; or the "Healthy Forests Initiative" affecting millions of acres within our national forests, which is nothing more than a government-subsidized timber sale in sensitive roadless areas; or the relentless push to drill for oil in the Arctic National Wildlife Refuge. I want to howl from the top of the mesa where we live, call friends, light fires, and dance wildly around them.

Not a wise thing to do in southern Utah.

It is difficult to find peace. I am torn between my anger and my empathy. And then I go for a walk. My balance returns. I calm down, breathe, and allow for deep listening to occur. Senator Bob Bennett listened. He disagreed. He responded. And he asked for more discussion.

I want to offer him the same courtesy, time, and respect.
I want to listen to what he has to say and why, and
answer with a thoughtful response.

Carlo Maria Martini, a member of the College of
Cardinals at the Vatican, in a letter to writer Umberto
Eco regarding the nature of democracy, wrote: "The delicate game of democracy provides for a dialectic
between opinions and beliefs in the hope that such
exchange will expand the collective moral conscience
that is the basis of orderly cohabitation."[7]

I begin to compose my letter, trying to articulate my
views with as much composure, fairness, and accuracy as
I can, making the best possible case for what I believe.

Dear Senator Bennett:

*Thank you for the generosity of your letter. Forgive
my delayed response. It has taken me weeks, months, to
sort through my thoughts and feelings regarding what you
have asked of me...*

*We do not agree on the war on Iraq. We do not agree
on the role of the United Nations, which I believe is essential if we are going to restore dignity and order to Iraq
through broad-based international coalitions. And we do
not agree on America's Redrock Wilderness Act currently
before the Senate. But I do believe we can come closer to
understanding why each of us is committed to our own
points of view and perhaps even adjust our perspectives
along the way to find creative alternatives that we cannot
only both live with, but feel comfortable in proposing*

together. These are the exchanges necessary to maintaining the open space of democracy…

I would like to propose an exchange program between us. I was thinking how our points of views might expand, even change, if we were to accompany each other to these areas of conflict. I would visit Iraq with you to witness the situation in Baghdad through your eyes and then you would visit with me areas now open for oil and gas exploration in Utah (once held as wilderness study areas before being released by Governor Leavitt and Secretary of the Interior Norton last April). Both are regions in need of creative discourse. Both are sites of deep philosophical divisions. Would these field trips interest you? I would like to think that we could bring our imaginations to the table and find a way through our positions to possibilities.

If you and I, a senator and a writer, but first, as neighbors, could find our way to common ground through shared experiences, perhaps it could provide an example of how people can come to listen to one another with real, authentic exchanges. I have always held the image of our founding fathers close to my heart, how they dared to disagree passionately with one another, yet remained open to what each had to say, some even changing their minds, as they forged our Constitution. This is the bedrock of our evolving republic…

Senator Bennett, you asked me a critical question in your letter, one I have pondered for months: What am I willing to die for?

Before the war in Iraq, thousands of Americans turned

to poetry to voice their opposition to the invasion, creating
the largest written protest in the history of this country.
Eleven thousand poems were presented to Congress on
March 5, 2003, by Sam Hamill and W. S. Merwin. My
words were simple ones:

The erosion of speech is the build-up of war.
Silence no longer supports prayers, but lives inside
the open mouths of the dead.[8]

After much thought, what I would be willing to die
for, and give my life to, is the freedom of speech. It is the
open door to all other freedoms.

We are a nation at war with ourselves. Until we
can turn to one another and offer our sincere words as to
why we feel the way we do with an honest commitment to
hear what others have to say, we will continue to project
our anger on the world in true, unconscious acts of terror.

Please know how much I appreciate the honesty and
thoughtfulness of your letter, the gesture of time spent on
the page with sincere regard for our differences as you
expressed your concrete ideas and beliefs. I have to believe
this is a foreign policy we might make more common within our own state of Utah.

I look forward to our ongoing conversation.

Respectfully yours,
TERRY TEMPEST WILLIAMS

—

Democracy invites us to take risks. It asks that we vacate the comfortable seat of certitude, remain pliable, and act, ultimately, on behalf of the common good. Democracy's only agenda is that we participate and that the majority voice be honored. It doesn't matter whether an answer is right or wrong, only that ideas be heard and discussed openly.

We are nothing but whiners if we are not willing to put our concerns and convictions on the line with a willingness to honestly listen and learn something beyond our own assumptions. Something new might emerge through shared creativity. If we cannot do this, I fear we will be left talking with only like-minded people, spending our days mumbling in the circles of the mad. I recall the words of William Faulkner, "What do we stand to lose? Everything."[9]

How we choose to support a living democracy will determine whether it will survive as the beating heart of a republic or merely be preserved as a withered artifact of a cold and ruthless empire.

"Fear and silence and spiritual isolation must be fought today,"[10] wrote Albert Camus in his essay "Neither Victims nor Executioners" in 1946, one year after World War II ended. I believe his words are contemporary. We can ask ourselves within the context and specificity of our own lives, how fear can be transformed into courage, silence transformed into honest expression, and spiritual isolation quelled through a sense of community.

Politics may be a game of power and money to those who have it, but for those of us who don't, politics is the public vehicle by which we exercise our voices within a democratic society.

At the end of Camus's essay, he states, "He who bases his hopes on human nature is a fool, he who gives up in the face of circumstances is a coward. And henceforth, the only honorable course will be to stake everything on a formidable gamble: that words are more powerful than munitions."[11]

To commence. To begin.

To comment. To discuss.

To commend. To praise and entrust.

To commit to the open space of democracy is to begin to make room for conversations that can move us toward a personal diplomacy. By personal diplomacy, I mean a flesh-and-blood encounter with public process that is not an abstraction but grounded in real time and space with people we have to face in our own hometowns. It's not altogether pleasant and there is no guarantee as to the outcome. Boos and cheers come in equal measure.

If we cannot engage in respectful listening there can be no civil dialogue and without civil dialogue we the people will simply become bullies and brutes, deaf to the truth that we are standing on the edge of a political chasm that is beginning to crumble. We all stand to lose ground. Democracy is an insecure landscape.

Do we dare to step back—stretch—and create an arch of understanding?

Self/Dawn

GROUND TRUTHING

GROUND TRUTHING: *The use of a ground survey to confirm findings of aerial imagery or to calibrate quantitative aerial observations; validation and verification techniques used on the ground to support maps; walking the ground to see for oneself if what one has been told is true; near surface discoveries.*

T HE ARCTIC IS BALANCING on an immense mirror. The water table is visible. Pools of light gather: lakes, ponds, wetlands. The tundra is shimmering. One squints perpetually.

—

Beauty is presence and it resides in the Brooks Range. My fear of flying in a small plane (I am riding on the back of a moth through clouds) is overcome by awe as we maneuver through majesty. These are not mountains but ramparts of raw creation. The retreat of gods. Crags, cirques, and glaciers sing hymns to ice. Talus slopes in grays and taupes become the marbled papers, creased and folded, inside prayer books. We fly through the valleys, following the river, watching the paths of Dall sheep baste one hillside to the next.

We land on a gravel bar, stopping just short of the raging river; our pilot, Dirk Nickisch from Coyote Air, lives up to the name of his company. Our guide Jim Campbell, his son, Kyle, my husband, Brooke, and I unload the plane quickly. Big weather is coming and six others in our party are waiting in Arctic Village to be picked up.

The plane makes a quick, short turnaround, speeds down the gravel bar, and lifts up—again missing the river in the nick of time. Dirk vanishes into the Brooks like a star engulfed by clouds. The sound of his engine disappears. We are left standing in deep, vast stillness, even with rushing water at our feet.

—

A semipalmated plover cries to distract us from her scrape in the stones holding three eggs between two channels of the river.

We move quickly off the gravel bar, wading across the swift river, struggling to find the shallowest point, then grab our gear and set up camp.

—

Dwarf fireweed creates flames of fuchsia on the riverbank. A soft gray ceiling of clouds brushes over our heads. I keep turning around to feel the embrace of these sweeping valleys. First thoughts: Never have I felt so safe. No development. No distractions. Nothing to break my heart. I was not prepared for this uninterrupted peace.

—

In the glare of the Marsh Fork, I think of the native people who have inhabited the northeast corner of Alaska for ten thousand years: the Iñupiat, along the Arctic coast; the Athabascan, south of the Brooks Range. I think of Trimble Gilbert, the fiddler, minister, and elder of the Gwich'in People, whom I met earlier today in Arctic Village. Our encounter is still vivid:

It is the Fourth of July. An American flag hangs vertically from the wooden beam of the general store. "It's Indian Sovereignty Day," Gilbert says, smiling. "Fireworks are planned." We sit on a bench outside the church in the center of the village. People are preparing for the celebration by setting up tables and starting the cook fires. Gilbert has just returned from Washington, D.C., lobbying on behalf of the Arctic National Wildlife Refuge.

"I go there more than I want," he says, "but I know my way around." He stands up and looks toward the taiga. "You know, this is the first year the caribou have gone the other direction." He turns around and points toward their traditional migratory path.

"Do you know why?" I ask.

He shakes his head. "But we're watching and wondering."

—

Drinking from the river—I am drinking from the river—this tincture of glaciers, this press of ice warmed by the sun. If water can pool in one's heart, then my heart is full. My arid heart has been waiting for decades, maybe three, for the return of the childhood pleasure of drinking directly from the source.

Drinking from the river. We all are. Ten pilgrims unaided, no iodine, no fancy filters or pumps, just the sweet dip of our cups from river to mouth, as much as we want, whenever we want. Our deep, unmeasured thirsts are quelled.

When my father asks me what it was like to visit the Arctic National Wildlife Refuge, I will simply say, "We drank from the river."

—

Deep dreams. We awake to the distress cries of a lesser yellowlegs. For two hours, this bird is relentless. I finally resort to counting: ninety cries per minute. Brooke and I get up to see if we are camped near its nest, but find nothing.

We walk the tundra behind us, up its terraces and steppes. We find bear tracks, caribou tracks, and a family of northern shrikes. We are bathed in light, endless light, sometimes volatile, ever changing. We watch weather as one watches fire.

—

Experience opens us, creates a chasm in our heart, an expansion in our lungs, allowing us to pull in fresh air to all that was stagnant. We breathe deeply and remember fear for what it is—a resistance to the unknown.

—

We travel by river on the Marsh Fork—a braided river. Nothing is easy here. We keep jumping in and out of the raft, walking the boat through shallow water, throwing our bodies back in before the deeper, swifter water carries us downriver. In and out. Once in the proper channel, we float. I enter a trance; the mantra of mountains rises, range after range of naked rock and peaks. I have no sense of time or scale, simply note this dynamic world that is both still and passing.

Our boat hits a rock. I am jolted back into life. There is little room for mistakes here. Around the bend we encounter *aufeis* (German for frozen river water) ten feet high, several hundred feet across. At its edge are translucent bands of turquoise. A cold wind bites. We paddle hard, careful not to be pulled into the current that has undercut the ice dam that would lure us into a cavern of cold, blue death. Carol Kasza, our guide, gives us commands. "A couple of strokes—two more, that's good." And then we lift our paddles back into the boat and glide.

—

An eagle's nest has fallen from the cliff's edge, crushed by a rockfall.

Each day, another layer of the self sloughs off, another layer of pretense erodes.

—

Knife-edged peaks split open the bellies of clouds. It rains. A long, cold storm has driven us into our tents. It is a day of stories told with our hands wrapped around cups of coffee and tea. We take our turn in the listening and the telling.

The range of topics is wide: insects we have loved; politicians we have loathed; tales of foolishness and valor. We see each other more fully and relax.

A moose cow and calf splash across the water.

—

Wolverine tracks. Wildness stamped on black sand. Wolverine tracks following caribou. It is a quick gait, a low-to-the-ground intensity. Five toes, claws exposed, heel pad predominant. Broad and round, the tracks measure from the tip of my middle finger to the ball of my palm.

I recall Adolph Murie once saying the hind feet step in the front-foot tracks, leaving a trail like that of a man walking.[12]

On hands and knees, I smell musk. I stand up and scan the hillside of dwarf birch and willow. Nothing. Nothing but stillness, my own awareness now hungry for movement.

—

Rock People appear along the beach. It is Brooke's obsession with standing stones. They are perfectly balanced, one on top of the other. Each assumes its own power and personality. He has enlisted our group and overnight, a tribe has gathered. They tell us how high the river is rising and when it drops, how swift the current is when a figure falls. At each camp, they are our silent companions. And for a time, we believe we are more than the few that we are in this vast arena of earth and sky.

What is it about this landscape that inspires, even directs, this kind of anthropomorphic architecture? To the Inuit, *inuksuit* are the enigmatic standing stones that dot the Arctic landscape. In translation, the word means "that which acts in the capacity of a human."[13] Many were built by their ancestors with strong intentions. They can direct caribou into the hands of hunters. They can guide those lost in treeless terrain, especially through a blizzard. They can mark the threshold of sacred space.

The land speaks to us through gestures. What we share as human beings is so much more than what separates us.

If we listen to the land, we will know what to do.

—

Clear skies after three days of steady rain. The color blue is electric. Amy Campion is break dancing on the tundra, spinning on top of her head. Now, in a hand-stand, she rolls down to her belly, then twirls on her back, her legs leading the rest of her body around and around. She is a student at UCLA. Her father, Tom, runs a hip clothing store for skateboarders. Pre-servation is his passion. A good portion of what he makes in profits goes to protecting the Arctic. The river is rushing behind her. The Earth is spinning. She is spinning. Joy enters the landscape. Tom watches his daughter. Amy's eyes are closed. How would we know the velocity of influence if there were no children to show us?

———

Along the gravel bar is a thin, gray stone. It catches my eye and I pick it up. The stone splits into thirds and invites me to play. The three pieces can be many things: When placed on the sand vertically, they become a Roman numeral III; when the middle one is removed and placed on top of the other two, it creates the symbol π —or the gateway to a Japanese temple. A triangle can be made. Take away the bottom line and allow it to become a vertical one, slightly beneath where the other two meet, and an arrow pointing north appears. The arrow pointing north is now a heron track walking south. I blink, and without moving the three fragments for a third time, I see a figure seeking shelter.

—

Our niece, Abby, who is accompanying us, has just graduated from Brown University with a degree in engineering. This is the first time she has had this kind of open space in her life for a good long while. I watch her in her solitude, taking in the vistas, learning the names of plants, her self-reliance in putting up her tent when the wind is trying to take it down. She is strong and secure in her reserve.

This morning, she carries a large rust-and-black caterpillar into camp. We find the creature in *A Naturalist's Guide to the Arctic* by E. C. Pielou. Sure enough, as we expected, it is an Arctic wooly bear (*Gynaephora groenlandica*). What we didn't expect was to learn it lives as a caterpillar for up to fourteen years, freezing solid each winter. Then, each spring, the caterpillar thaws and resumes its life where it left off the previous summer.

"Think antifreeze," Abby says, always interested in structure and design.

When the caterpillar matures, it pupates into a cocoon, emerging as an adult moth. The moth is not so long lived. Its purpose is simply to reproduce, which it does quickly, and the lifecycle begins all over again.

The smallest of lives here in the Arctic are miraculous.

Whether it is the wooly bear that lives over a decade, much of its life in a deep freeze, or the warble flies and nose bots that burrow into the hide of the caribou to stay warm, each life is perfectly adapted to the perils of extreme cold.

We release the wooly bear. Its undulating body on many legs finds its place back in the bush. Abby looks at me, impressed and amused. "Just don't try to sell me on the virtues of mosquitoes," she says, putting her head net on before sitting down for breakfast.

—

It is a day of walking. Most decide to climb an unnamed peak. Cindy Shogan and I choose a more modest hike where we can find a vantage point to watch animals. To our great surprise, our attention focuses not on big mammals, but poppies.

We are on our bellies for a ground squirrel's look. Tissuelike petals form a yellow cup that literally holds light which translates to heat as the flowers turn their heads to continuously follow the sun. The blossom is supported on a threadlike stem. The poppies we meet have survived the pounding rains and brutal winds of the past three days. Not a petal is torn or tattered. They simply raise their heads toward the sun and lure in flies with the seduction of warmth. In return, the flies pollinate the poppies.

Cindy and I hardly move all day, engrossed in the mosaic of vegetation reminiscent of the Unicorn Tapestries with their myriad flowers. We turn our binoculars bottom lens up and use them as magnifying glasses: purple saxifrages, moss campion, dryad, cinquefoil, bistort, death camas, cloud berries, blueberries, and Labrador tea. Reindeer lichen is ubiquitous. Within the leaves of lupine rest single drops of water like diamonds.

After our tundra crawl, we find an outcropping of rocks that overlooks one of the hanging valleys above the river. Cindy, the executive director of the Alaska Wilderness League, is one of the smartest strategists of her generation. She talks about the political challenges presented by the Bush administration and their relentless drive to drill for oil in the Arctic National Wildlife Refuge.

I ask her what she fears most. Ever the optimist, Cindy says, "We're not going to lose the Arctic, it's just the opposition's endless bombardment and trickery." Alaska's senior senator, Ted Stevens, head of the powerful Appropriations Committee, is now planning to attach his drilling proposal to any piece of legislation that can be bought, from energy to transportation.

This is Cindy's first trip to the refuge. We are here to see the lands left in limbo, coldly referred to in Washington as "the 1002" (ten-o-two), a number referring to a particular amendment which says that these 1.2 million acres within the Arctic National Wildlife Refuge could be opened for oil and gas development. These disputed lands are part of the Coastal Plain, where the great caribou migrations occur—the long sweep of land that stretches from the foothills of the Brooks Range to the Beaufort Sea.

Cindy and I discuss the story of Subhankar Banerjee, a gifted young photographer from India who quit his job, cashed in his savings in 2000, and has been taking pictures of the Arctic ever since. He recently published a book titled *Arctic National Wildlife Refuge: Seasons of Life and Land*.[14]

In March 2003, during the budget debate, Senator Barbara Boxer introduced an amendment to prevent consideration of drilling in the refuge from being added to the bill. She held Banerjee's book up on the Senate floor as an example of the elegance of this place and why it deserves protection. She then invited members to visit Mr. Banerjee's upcoming show at the Smithsonian Institution. Ted Stevens took note and said, "People who vote against this today are voting against me, and I will not forget it." Boxer's amendment passed anyway.

A few weeks later, the show Subhankar Banerjee had been promised by the Smithsonian, which was to hang in a central location near the rotunda, had suddenly been relegated to the basement. Evocative captions offering a rationale for conservation with quotations by Peter Matthiessen, David Allen Sibley, Jimmy Carter, and others had been removed and replaced with perfunctory labels such as "Buff-breasted Sandpiper: Coastal plain of the Jago River." A cry of foul play went out in Washington and in May 2003, Senator Richard Durbin used a

EXPLORE BOOKSELLERS
221 East Main Aspen, Colorado 925-5336

```
  317714 Reg 1 ID  45 1:08 pm 01/04/05
S BB CLASSIC SKETCH   1 @  13.95    13.95
S OPEN SPACE OF DEM   1 @   8.00     8.00
SUBTOTAL                            21.95
TAX: city/cnty - 5.7%               1.25
TAX: state - 2.9%                     .64
TOTAL SALES TAX                      1.89
TOTAL                               23.84
VISA PAYMENT                        23.84
```

OPEN EVERY DAY OF THE YEAR
Please present this receipt for exchange
or store credit only.

hearing on the Smithsonian's budget to question whether outside influence had been used to move Subhankar's exhibition.

It was Cindy and the Alaska Wilderness League that placed a copy of Subhankar Banerjee's book in Senator Boxer's hands. It was also Cindy who nudged Senator Durbin[15] for an investigation. She did not tell me these facts. I had to find these details in the press.

Subhankar Banerjee has become, unwittingly, a celebrity photographer who bears the distinction of being censored by the United States government. For what? The threat of beauty.

In the open space of democracy, beauty is not optional, but essential to our survival as a species.

In a few days, we will reach the confluence of the Marsh Fork and the Canning River. The Canning is the fluid western boundary of the Arctic National Wildlife Refuge that determines where one can now drill and where one cannot. It will carry us into the heart of this national debate. Right now, the rallying cry and corruption of politics seem a world apart from the world we are in, because in the rock-hard, ice-sculpted reality of the Arctic—they are.

—

Arctic still life: A caribou antler, laced with lichen, orange and yellow, is wrapped around a dwarf willow

which now provides shade and shelter for what was
once held high in motion.

Cindy finds a piece of *quiviut*, musk ox hair, and hands
it to me.

What will we make of the life before us? How do we
translate the gifts of solitary beauty into the action
required for true participatory citizenship?

—

Brooks Yeager, Cindy's husband, has just come down the
mountain with Brooke and Abby. He was assistant secretary for policy in the Department of the Interior during the Clinton administration, when he labored long
and hard on behalf of the Arctic. He has tender eyes and
this trip for him, as it is for all of us, is a "ground
truthing" to see if what he has fought for and imagined
is true. I believe it has taken him the longest to surren-
der to Arctic time. He is quick-witted, disciplined, and
discriminating, aware of acreage, drainages, and dis-
tances. He knows firsthand how politics translates into
policy and how much is bargained away in bills before
Congress.

He is the keeper of the bird count: thirty-nine species.
He saw a merlin today; the rest of us missed it.

—

More rain. More stories. They pop open like umbrellas. Jim, tall and lean, with gray, cropped hair and large, skilled hands, crouches down over the stove to make coffee. He knows wilderness intimately, the wilderness of war and the wilderness of peace. For more than twenty years, he has traversed the Brooks Range by foot, run its rivers, and camped night after night in the buoyancy of the tundra.

He tells of coming home from Vietnam in 1968, walking into his father's tavern in Pennsylvania, still in uniform, completely disoriented. A few weeks later, he found himself holding the security line in Chicago at the Democratic Convention and fighting the antiwar protesters. "Nothing made sense," he says. "Nothing." And then, just a year or so ago, he attended a ceremony for Vietnam veterans in Fairbanks, Alaska. "Welcome home," a woman said to him. Jim paused, holding back emotion. "It was the first time I had heard those words."

Light shifts. An opening is created. We step outside the cook tent and place four topographical maps that encompass the 19.5 million acres of the Arctic National Wildlife Refuge on the ground to see where we are and where we are going. We will cover another ten to fifteen miles on the river today. In a week, we will be camping on the Coastal Plain.

—

Scale cannot be registered here in human terms. It is
geologic, tectonic, and planetary. Stegosauraslike ridge-
lines form the boundaries of our passage. Ribbonlike
waterfalls cascade for miles down cliffs. What I thought
was a swallow became an eagle. Weather changes minute
by minute. Gray tumultuous clouds weave themselves
into patterns of herringbone, yet a strange softness abides,
even in the razor-cut terror of this rugged terrain.

—

Coming into the confluence where the Marsh Fork
meets the Canning feels celebratory. It is a great flood-
ing, far and wide. Blinding light ricochets off platinum
strands of water. Braided rivers, braided energies. Wild
waters intertwine. We pull the boat over a few rock gar-
dens until we find the deeper channels. The roots of sil-
ver-leafed willows, exposed in the cut bank, tremble like
the nervous system of the Arctic.

—

I cannot sleep and slip from the comfort of our tent to face the low, diffused glow of midnight. All colors bow to the gentle arc of light the sun creates as it strolls across the horizon. Green steppes become emerald. The river, lapis. A patch of cotton grass ignites. My eyes catch the illumined wings of a tern, an Arctic tern, fluttering, foraging above the river—the embodiment of grace, suspended. The tern animates the vast indifference with its own vibrant intelligence. Black cap; blood-red beak pointed down; white body with black-tipped wings. With my eyes laid bare, I witness a bright thought in big country. While everyone is sleeping, the presence of this tern hovering above the river, alive, alert, engaged, becomes a vision of what is possible.

On this night, I met the Arctic Angel and vowed the 22,000 miles of her migratory path between the Arctic and Antarctica would not be in vain. I will remember her. No creature on Earth has spent more time in daylight than this species. No creature on Earth has shunned darkness in the same way as the Arctic tern. No creature carries the strength and delicacy of determination on its back like this slight bird. If air is the medium of the Spirit, then the Arctic tern is its messenger.

What I know is this: When one hungers for light it is only because one's knowledge of the dark is so deep.

—

It is a well-worn path made by grizzlies. No, that is not quite right. They are the ancient footsteps of bears. Bear after bear has stepped in the same paw prints as preceding bears. These bear steps sink into the tundra, circle the rock, and disappear. The large rock, a glacial erratic, is covered in fur rubbed from the backs of bears. The weight from the bears has pressed the tundra down to the permafrost. The steps are deep and wet, and cold. This place is holy.

A grizzly has just circled the rock. Tom spotted him first from the river. We stop, tie down our boats, and hike to a knoll where we can watch from a safe distance, separated by a ravine. The grizzly is pawing the ground for roots. The bear is oblivious to us. We are not oblivious of the bear. We sit down and eat lunch, mindful of where and how the grizzly is moving. An upland sandpiper cries, circles us, and raises her wings as she lands. Light breaks through clouds and catches the bear's honey-colored coat, with a brown line traveling down his hump and back. His massive body, moving in all its undulating power, makes my blood quiver. I note his small eyes, his large head, and the length of his claws, perfect for digging. Another hour flies. We eat and watch as he eats and saunters. The wind shifts, the bear looks up, stands, and sniffs the air. We freeze. He turns and runs downhill.

—

It is called "Bear Shaman"—an Iñupiat sculpture carved out of soapstone. At one end is Man, crouched close to the earth. At the other end is Bear, in search of prey. Both Man and Bear live inside the same body. Their shared heart determines who will be seen and who will disappear. Shape-shifting is its own form of survival.

—

I find a feather of a snowy owl, brush my face with its soft white webbing, and leave it on the ground. Where are they?

—

For several days, we have been floating the Canning River. In the end, we will have covered almost 125 miles. We are now camped on the famed 1002 lands. On one side of the river is the Arctic National Wildlife Refuge. On the other side are the Alaska state lands where oil and gas exploration is underway. Keep walking west and you'll bump into Prudhoe Bay.

I thought I saw a musk ox across the river. It was an empty oil drum.

———

This windswept country is so revealing that you see what you are spiritually, morally.

—Benjamin Wyer Bragonier[16]

———

The Arctic is made up of dreams. And not everyone's is the same. My dream of the Arctic National Wildlife Refuge was planted in my heart by Mardy Murie. The year was 1974. The place was Moose, Wyoming, at the Murie Ranch where the famed naturalists, Olaus and Adolph, with their wives, Mardy and Louise, made their home at the base of the Tetons.

I was a student at the Teton Science School. I was eighteen years old. Mardy introduced us to Alaska through her stories of growing up in Fairbanks, of Olaus's field work studying caribou for the U.S. Fish and Wildlife Service in 1920. She showed us her slides of their summer on the Sheenjek River in 1956 with Olaus, Brina Kessel, Bob Krear, and George Schaller. She shared with us their dream of Arctic protection, and the dedication of their group of friends, including Bob Marshall, Ed Zahnhiser, George Collins, Lowell Sumner, Starker Leopold, writers Sigurd Olson and Lois Crisler, and Supreme Court Justice William O. Douglas, along with local conservationists Celia Hunter and Ginny Wood, who helped build a state and national constituency for the creation of the Arctic National Wildlife Range, placing pressure on Congress until it was created in 1960.

Revolutionary patience. This community of Americans never let go of their wild, unruly faith that love can lead to social change. The Muries believed that the protection of wildlands was the protection of natural processes, the unseen presence in wilderness. The Wilderness Act, another one of their dreams, was signed in 1964.

It was Mardy who inspired me to join her and a thousand others on June 5, 1977, to attend the Alaska Lands Hearings in Denver, Colorado. I hitched a ride with friends; we slept on the floor of a church. The next morning, road weary, we cleaned ourselves up and found seats inside the capitol building. This was one of the many regional hearings conducted by the House Interior Subcommittee on General Oversight and Alaskan Lands.

Those who wanted to offer testimony signed up. Mardy was among the first to be called forward. I remember her white braided hair, her poise, her strength. Her love of Alaska transcended her words.

When she stood before the presiding congressman, Representative John Seiberling, her whole history and community stood with her.

"I am testifying as an emotional woman," I can still remember her saying, "and I would like to ask you, gentlemen, what's wrong with emotion?"

Perhaps she was remembering the emotion in Olaus's voice when he testified before the Senate two decades earlier and said:

We long for something more, something that has a mental, a spiritual impact on us. This idealism, more than anything else, will set us apart as a nation striving for something worthwhile in the universe....It is inevitable, if we are to progress as people in the highest sense, that we shall become ever more concerned with the saving of the intangible resources, as embodied in this move to establish the Arctic Wildlife Range.[17]

—

I have held this dream of visiting the Arctic for thirty years. That the refuge has become a symbol for how we define our national priorities is a testament to its innate power. That it continues to survive, resist, and absorb our own greed and economic tensions, year after year, is evidence of the force of love that has protected these wildlands for generations.

As the Brooks Range recedes behind us, I am mindful that Mardy is approaching 101 years of age. She has never shed her optimism for wild Alaska. I am half her age and Abby is half of mine. We share her passion for this order of quiet freedom. America's wildlands are vulnerable and they will always be assailable as long as what we value in this nation is measured in monetary terms, not spiritual ones. What are we willing to give our lives to if not the perpetuation of the sacred? Can we continue to stand together in our collective wisdom and say, these particular lands are inviolable, deserving protection by law and the inalienable right of safe passage for all beings that dwell here? Wilderness designation is the promise of this hope held in trust.

The open space of democracy provides justice for all living things—plants, animals, rocks, and rivers, as well as human beings.

———

The Arctic is a landscape where migrating birds create blizzards with feathers, where polar bears walk on water, and where white owls circle solitary men, reminding them of their limitations. Here, it is not unusual for wolves to walk up to children to hear the words spoken by humans; or to find a piece of stone carved in the shape of a whale.

This is not magic, only the nature of a landscape observed.

—

Love is nurtured through time. Time is what we lack. On the Canning River, time is all we have.

Reflection is part of the liturgy of this landscape. Repetition of forms—rock, ice, water, a leaf print that appears as a fossil—creates a devotion of relief, the truth of sequential experience.

A willow ptarmigan on the riverbank still wears winter white as she molts toward summer brown.

—

Sun. Hot flashes? Our tent is so hot, I am burning up. I rip off my clothes, unzip our tent, pull on my boots, and do a mad sprint across the tundra, down to the river, and jump in. There is so much heat coming off my body, the frigid water doesn't faze me. The aufeis is just a few feet away.

It is glorious seeing the world upside down as I drop my head down to dry my hair. Two glaucous gulls stand on the ice—white on white.

A few seconds later, upriver, I hear, "Man, there's some heat in that sun! Goddamn!" And there stands another naked figure in the river. Male.

—

Gravel beds—literally; we sleep on the riverbank. What we are meant to do: work hard, play hard, eat, make love, rest, sleep. I walk ahead in my own midday trance and find another shelf of aufeis. Being from the desert, it is the ice that intrigues me. The crystals on its leading edge belong to chandeliers. I run my fingers across them. They fall like musical glass notes and awaken my friends.

—

We now stand on the Coastal Plain, and it is easy to imagine Kansas before settlement. So much sky and the endless horizon.

Mosquitoes are thick—each of us has our own attentive cloud.

We are camped on Shublik Island, another part of the 1002 lands, what Cindy and Brooks call "the soul of the Arctic." Cindy has the maps out, looking at Red Hill and the miles we paddled yesterday on the river, close to twenty-five. It was a long, arduous day and our muscles ache.

———

A fragrance drifts across the Canning. Without thought, each of us begins breathing deeply. Sighs emerge on the exhale. We are being drugged by perfume. An innocence is wafting on the wind. I am weeping and I don't know why. Brooke stands up in our boat and points. The plains are magenta all the way to the horizon, a blanket of petals, pink and violet variations of wild sweet pea.[18]

———

When I ask Carol to describe the Arctic National Wildlife Refuge in one word, she doesn't hesitate. "Wholeness," she says. I am in the back of the boat with her as she steers us ahead to our last camp.

"It's not just the refuge or ANWR, the 1002, the National Petroleum Reserve Area, or any of the other throwaway names that are being bantered about in Washington," she explains, "but the entire region of what lives and breathes in the shadow of the Brooks Range

with all its peaks and valleys, braided rivers, and coast-
lines. It's this layered sense of wilderness, the uninterrupted vistas without man's hand on it.

"If we choose to continue to only focus on particular
areas, then this whole region becomes part of an intellectual and political project of fragmentation. Do we
have to keep cutting it up into smaller and smaller bits
and pieces until we finally call it a compromise? The
Arctic National Wildlife Refuge is already a compromise—it was in 1960 and again in 1980."

Carol, a woman in her fifties, is as fierce and wise and
beautiful as the lines that give her face expression. She is
a woman who has made her work her passion and has
brought her whole family into her explorer's heart. She
and Jim run Arctic Treks together. They now include
their son, Kyle, who is rowing one of the three boats on
this trip.

"I want to hear a different discussion," she says. "I want
people to ask, 'How does it feel to be in this country?
What do you remember here that you have otherwise
forgotten? Why do we want to destroy or diminish anything that inspires us to live more honestly?'"

—

The sanctity of solitude: I sit above a lake after a long
walk up the steppe and then north across the tundra.

Two swans are mirrored in the water. Flocks of sand-pipers fly in and out of the tussocks. Each bird weighs barely an ounce.

A long-tailed jaeger sits next to me. I try not to move. With my legs crossed and my eyes barely open, I enter the space of meditation.

A wolf howls. My body leaps. The jaeger flies. Fear floods my heart. Presence creates presence. I am now alert. To feel yourself prey is to be shocked back into the reality of the Arctic's here and now.

—

This is what I have learned in these short weeks in the refuge:

You cannot afford to make careless mistakes, like med-itating in the presence of wolves, or topping your boots in the river, or losing a glove, or not securing your tent down properly. Death is a daily occurrence in the wild, not noticed, not respected, not mourned. In the Arctic, I've learned ego is as useless as money.

Choose one's traveling companions well. Physical strength and prudence are necessary. Imagination and ingenuity are our finest traits.

Expect anything.

You can change your mind like the weather.

Patience is more powerful than anger. Humor is more

attractive than fear.

Pay attention. Listen. We are most alive when discovering.

Humility is the capacity to see.

Suffering comes, we do not have to create it.

We are meant to live simply.

We are meant to be joyful.

Life continues with and without us.

Beauty is another word for God.

—

Today is Tom Campion's birthday. He is 55 years old. He is mastering the art of whittling his life down to what is essential. We are here because of his generosity. He wanted us to see the Arctic for ourselves. This is his party.

In a serious moment, Tom says who he is and all he stands for is a result of what he has experienced in wildness. "Even the love I have for my children."

We celebrate with a hidden keg of Grolsch, carefully packed by Jim. Brooks delivers a rousing toast. Gifts are offered: a silver kite; a turquoise bear; a poem read by Kyle; a birthday cake with candles and a song.

—

Abby and I wash dishes down by the river. Amy joins us. I look at these beautiful young women, so strong and creative, unwilling to settle for comfort and security over substance and desire. An engineer. A dancer. Where will their lives take them? What will they remember of these days inside the refuge?

———

Here is my question: what might a different kind of power look like, feel like? And can power be distributed equitably among ourselves, even beyond our own species?

———

The power of nature is the power of a life in association. Nothing stands alone. On my haunches, I see a sunburst lichen attached to limestone; algae and fungi are working together to break down rock into soil. I cannot help but recognize a radical form of democracy at play. Each organism is rooted in its own biological niche, drawing its power from its relationship to other organisms. An equality of being contributes to an ecological state of health and succession.

"We can only attain harmony and stability by con-sulting ensemble,"[19] writes Walt Whitman. This is my definition of community, and community interaction is the white-hot center of a democracy that burns bright.

Within the refuge, if I rotate slowly in place, what I see is a circumference of continuity. What I feel is a spir-itual cohesion born out of wholeness. It is organic, cellu-lar. I am at home in the peace of an intact world. The open space of democracy is not interested in hierarchies but in networks and systems where power is circular, not linear; a power reserved not for an entitled few, but shared and maintained by many. Public lands are our public commons and they belong to everyone. We enter these sacred lands soulfully and remember what it is we have forgotten—the gift of time and space. The Arctic National Wildlife Refuge is the literal open space of democracy. The privilege of being here is met with the responsibility I feel to experience and express its com-pounding grace.

I think of the Arctic National Wildlife Refuge as a place of Original Mind, where the ongoing natural processes of life can continue without interference. Our evolutionary past and our future are secured here. This is a place where the press of humanity can be lift-ed in the name of restraint and where our species' magnanimous nature can be practiced. The Arctic be-comes a breathing space. In the company of wild nature, we experience our own humble core of dependency on the land.

I hear Walt Whitman's voice once again, "The quality of Being...is the lesson of Nature."[20] Raw, wild beauty is a deeply held American value. It is its own declaration of independence. Equality is experienced through humility. Liberty is expressed through the simple act of wandering.

———

Well after midnight, Brooke and I walk up a hillside blanketed in Arctic poppies and blue forget-me-nots. On the distant horizon across the Canning we can see a flare-up from Prudhoe Bay. A black column of smoke smears an apricot sky.

We look the other direction. Brooke spots a silver Arctic fox with the most exquisite black tail. Two parasitic jaegers are storming the fox with aerial loops and cries of terror. He jumps and snaps at the forked-tailed birds. They fly higher and hover above him like black crossbows ready to strike. The fox spins around. The birds dive down and nip his ears. Sufficiently annoyed, he trots off. The jaegers calm down. We suspect a nest nearby.

The Arctic belongs to winter. No other. Summer simply borrows a few weeks for its love of the spectacle. In a manic rush, life exerts itself fully.

Golden plovers run in front of us. They turn. We are looking into the faces of pharaohs.

We walk for several hours along the tundra shelf, talking very little. Such joy. How do we return home without breaking these threads that bind us to life? How do we return our gratitude for all we have seen? We stop and lie on our backs, side by side, watching the clouds. A deep and abiding stillness passes through us. Our hands clasp.

—

3:00 a.m. Divine light. I am called out of the tent by the sun. I walk north, blinded by its radiance. On top of the ridge, I see two figures—human—Jim and Kyle. I wave. They wave back. Kyle raises his arms above his head with bent elbows. I understand. Caribou. I walk briskly up toward the men.

"Thousands upon thousands of caribou," Jim says. I turn. My binoculars scan the landscape for several minutes. Heads, antlers, backs, tails, legs, hooves, one caribou merges into another. Calves are jumping next to their mothers. It is an endless stream of animals walking across the tundra. Without field glasses, they register as a heat wave. I cannot take my eyes off them.

Jim and Kyle walk down to the flats and wake everyone. One by one, they rise from their tents. They rise to a rainbow, and another. A double rainbow is arching over the plains in Arctic light and we watch, as human beings have always watched, the great herds in motion.

Gathering

ENGAGEMENT

I T IS UNUSUALLY STILL. I am standing in Mardy and Olaus Murie's living room in Moose, Wyoming. It is the first time I have entered their home since Mardy passed away on October 19, 2003. She was 101 years old.

My eyes travel around the cabin and see Olaus's paintings of caribou migration still hanging above the east window. Their Alaskan library is intact. And the rawhide lamps are where they have always been on either side of the couch.

On the far wall is a piece of calligraphy, the words Mardy spoke at the Jackson Hole High School commencement in 1974: "Give yourself the adventure of doing what you can do, with what you have, even if you have nothing but the adventure of trying. How much better than standing in a corner with your back to the wall."

I am standing in the corner with my back to the wall. Never have I felt such dismay over the leadership and public policies of our nation. Never have I felt such determination and faith in our ability to change our country's current direction. How to reconcile these seemingly contradictory emotions in an election year when we appear to be anything but united states?

Snow is banked against the windows, melting. Last night, there was a conversation between great gray owls on the ranch. I think of all the conversations that took place in the warmth of this log home in the middle of the Tetons; imagine the stories told, the secrets shared, and the strategies developed to safeguard wildlands in this country. I recall the cups of tea poured and the plates of cookies passed at my own visits and how I always left believing what was possible, never doubting what was not.

The Muries and their circle of friends challenged the ethical structure of the United States government and institutions such as the U.S. Fish and Wildlife Service. Olaus and his brother, Adolph, changed the public's perception of predators through their research on coyotes in Yellowstone and wolves in Denali. Olaus supported his colleague Rachel Carson when she was under fire from the Department of Agriculture following the publication of *Silent Spring.* Mardy campaigned endlessly for the protection of wild Alaska.

The Muries changed laws and made new ones, even the Wilderness Act of 1964.

A Presidential Medal of Freedom is perched on the mantel of their stone fireplace. I remember when Mardy was given this honor by President Clinton in the White House on January 15, 1998,[21] how he knelt down and placed the medallion around her neck. She was in a wheelchair, frail but present. Those of us in attendance, family and friends who witnessed this ceremony, saw her tears. I wanted to ask her what she was thinking in that moment, but I didn't. It felt private.

What I wish I could ask Mardy now is, how do we engage in the open space of democracy in times of terror?

I believe she would send me home.

———

Castle Valley is a small desert community in southeastern Utah. Large cottonwood trees shadow the creeks that flow from the high country down through the juniper, piñon, and sage. The Colorado River creates its northern boundary; the LaSal Mountains rise to the south; Castleton Tower stands to the east, next to a geologic formation locals call "The Priest and Nuns"; and Porcupine Rim runs due west. The town is surrounded by 9,000 acres of Utah School Institutional Trust Lands, the blue squares that appear on state maps across the American West like a checkerboard. These school trust lands were created at statehood by the U.S. Congress with the understanding that they could be sold to generate income for education. And beyond the trust lands, three wilderness study areas frame the valley: Morning Glory, Mary Jane, and Fisher Towers. The valley now supports around three hundred residents. If you drive in for a visit you will be greeted by a sign that says, "CAUTION: FALLING SKY."

Brooke and I moved to Castle Valley from Salt Lake City in the fall of 1998. The silence was both welcome and unsettling. The wind was a constant reminder that this erosional landscape is still in motion. The only thing we found we could count on was changing weather—

the extreme heat of summer and extreme cold in winter. Fall and spring were seasons aligned with heaven. The daily tides of deer became our cue to when we awoke and when we retired. Our neighbors were both warm and solitary. We all shared a love of quiet and a sense of community, within reason—people largely left each other alone.

In the spring of 1999, the Utah School Institutional Trust Lands Administration (SITLA) sold eighty acres at the base of Parriott Mesa at a public auction to a developer in Aspen with a partner in Moab, without proper notice to the community of Castle Valley. The developers assured the town that the land was bought for a dwelling for one of their daughters. But within a matter of weeks, a large FOR SALE sign was placed on wooden stilts and hammered into the red desert, the price of the land tripling. Parriott Mesa was now slated for a subdivision.

Castle Valley is not an affluent community. Most incomes fall below the national average. There was concern about what a high-end development would do to taxes and everyone knew water was a serious issue, with the Castle Valley aquifer dropping due to drought. The community panicked, and within days a meeting was called. The small adobe home belonging to Susan Ulery was packed with people: Mormons, non-Mormons, Republicans, Democrats, Libertarians, attorneys, carpenters, climbers, artists, teachers, and old hippies—the full range was in attendance.

We recognized Castleton Tower as the flame of America's Redrock Wilderness. We talked about how the ecological integrity of the Colorado River Corridor was at stake if the SITLA lands were to be developed; we acknowledged the hundreds of oil and gas leases that could be activated. We believed there had to be viable alternatives. Out of our shock, anger, and affection for each other, the Castle Rock Collaboration (CRC) was formed. We had no money. We had no power. We had only our shared love of home and a desire for dialogue with the open spaces that defined our town.

We wrote up an article of intention:

In the presence of Castleton Tower, we hereby create a covenant with these lands, that as good stewards we will commit ourselves to preserving and protecting the natural character of this valley as we seek to understand our own personal development as a community.

The Castle Rock Collaboration is an exercise in bed-rock democracy. We are dedicated to the process of listening to the land and each other, exploring what we want our future to be, working together to minimize the pressures of growth, ensuring the health and majesty of this pocket of peace we call home.

Meanwhile, under the cover of darkness, the large FOR SALE sign disappeared—only to reappear the next morning beneath Turret Arch inside Arches National Park, complete with telephone number. Shortly after dawn, both the developer and the Park Service received calls from numerous tourists enthusiastically interested in purchasing the arch. The developer was delighted, having thought he had missed something spectacular at the base of Parriott Mesa. The park rangers were baffled until they took a drive and saw the sign for themselves. Photographs were taken. The point was made. These developers would sell anything if they could, even our national parks.

The story rocked Castle Valley. Panic was replaced by humor. Nobody knew who did it; Coyote had entered town. This is, after all, Abbey's Country.

A few weeks later we learned that the developers were going to strip the land on Monday, May 24, 1999. But an anonymous donor came forward literally the day before the bulldozers were set to roll and wrote CRC a check. With the help of Utah Open Lands, we were able to make the developers an offer and buy back the eighty acres as our first act in the name of community trust.

Suddenly, the Castle Rock Collaboration was taken seriously.

We organized ourselves. Bill Viavant, a beloved elder in the valley, then in his late eighties, offered his home for monthly meetings. Paula and Eddie Morandi also opened their house to the community. Each person volunteered his or her best skills: Laura Kamala, a wildlife biologist who had lived in the valley for more than twenty years, offered to contact the Division of Wildlife Resources and help create maps identifying critical winter range for mule deer. Town council member Karen Nelson, who worked for the Synergy Company marketing vitamin supplements, was schooled in water issues. She agreed to begin research on the Castle Valley aquifer and watershed concerns. Alice Drogin, a former naturalist for Arches National Park who now runs a plant nursery with her husband Ken, volunteered to create a website. With Dave Erley's leadership, Kitty Calhoun, Jay Smith, Jack Tackle, and Greg Childs, world-class climbers who live in the valley, all agreed to engage fellow climbers in helping to raise money, knowing that the next block of land to be auctioned off was the 220 acres at the base of the desert climbing icon Castleton Tower. Bill Hedden, a former county commissioner and Utah director of the Grand Canyon Trust, with his wife Eleanor Bliss, volunteered to do research on SITLA and its relationship to other rural communities in Utah and find out exactly how much money actually trickles down to the schools.

Artists painted. Writers wrote. Attorneys agreed to review documents for potential legal snags, and photographers, like Tom Till from Moab, donated their images for posters that could be sold for revenue.

We sought the continued counsel of Utah Open Lands, which had a structure already in place and agreed to include CRC under its umbrella of local land trusts in the state, and to help us broker future land deals. We also sought partnerships with The Nature Conservancy and the Grand Canyon Trust to help us identify critical parcels for biological diversity.

Suddenly, we did not feel so powerless.

The leadership of CRC, Dave Erley, Laura Kamala, and Brooke Williams, along with Castle Valley's mayor, Bruce Keeler, met with Ric McBrier, the representative from SITLA, and asked him to enter a planning process with us. After arduous conversations, discussions, and on-the-ground field trips, SITLA finally agreed. They also agreed not to auction off any new parcels of land until the planning process was complete. Together, we hired a planning firm from Boulder, Colorado, that we both felt comfortable with to help lay out a strategy for responsible land use. Five years later, the process is still ongoing.

During this time, we found through shared research with The Nature Conservancy and botanist Joel Tuhy that two threatened and endangered plant species live on three parcels of SITLA terrain in the northern end of the valley: Jones cycladenia (*Cycladenia humilis* var. *jonesii*) and Schultz stickleaf (*Mentzelia shultziorum*). As a result, The Nature Conservancy secured these lands and identified them as crucial habitat for the rare species.

I remember taking a group of children in the valley up to see the endangered plants. We hiked the steep sandy slopes of Jello Hill, so named because of its unstable red scree. We searched for some time until we found a small patch of Schultz stickleaf, which grows nowhere else in the world. The children knelt down on hands and knees for a closer look. Each had a hand lens and moved the glass back and forth until it was perfectly focused. They didn't say much, they just wanted to keep looking at the delicate yellow petals and the diamond-shaped leaves against the barren slope. I believe it was the first time they had encountered something rare and fragile.

Members of the climbing community gave slide shows around the American West, educating audiences about the threat to Castleton Tower and surrounding wildlands. With the help of companies like Petzl, Patagonia, and Black Diamond, and through the support of The Access Fund, the Castle Rock Collaboration was able to raise the money necessary to purchase the wide sweep of land at the base of this sandstone spire.

And with the help of Jim Salmon, a Vietnam veteran and scout master for the Church of Jesus Christ of Latter-Day Saints, Laura Kamala and Wendy Fisher of Utah Open Lands persuaded the Division of Wildlife Resources that Castle Valley qualified for state funds to help purchase over five hundred acres of school trust lands in order to protect critical winter range for the mule deer at the southern end of the valley.

In the five years that we have been engaged in this process with SITLA, the Castle Rock Collaboration and its partners have protected over three thousand acres and raised nearly four million dollars. But perhaps the most important outcome has been the creation of an atmosphere of engagement with other committed individuals who live along the Colorado River Corridor, all part of a concerted conservation effort to create a long-term vision for the watershed now

referred to collectively as the Richardson's Amphi-
theater Land Protection Project.

There is still a tremendous amount of work to be
done—3,600 acres remain vulnerable to development at
the base of Round Mountain in the center of Castle Valley.
Bureau of Land Management parcels previously closed to
oil and gas leases are now open for business. And the
onslaught of thousands of off-road vehicles in Grand
County, playing war games on the slickrock, render another kind of violence to the desert. But we are learning that
a community engaged is a community empowered.

If we listen to the land, we will know what to do.

—

There is a particular juniper tree, not so far from our
house, that I sit under frequently. This tree shelters my
thoughts and brings harmony to mind. I consult this
tree by simply seeking its company. No words are spoken. Sensations come into my body and I recognize
this cellular awakening as an organic form of listening, the spiritual cohesion one feels in places like the
Arctic on such a grand scale. A throbbing intelligence
passes from this tree into my bloodstream and I
remember my animal body that has evolved alongside
my consciousness as a human being. This form of
engagement reveals familial ties and I honor this tree's

standing in the community. We share a pact of survival. I used to be embarrassed to speak of these things, my private correspondences with trees and birds and deer, for fear of seeming mad. But now, it seems mad not to speak of these things—our unspoken intimacies with Other.

Open lands open minds.

In the open space of democracy, we are listening—ears alert—we are watching—eyes open—registering the patterns and possibilities for engagement. Some acts are private; some are public. Our oscillations between local, national, and global gestures map the full range of our movement. Our strength lies in our imagination, and paying attention to what sustains life, rather than what destroys it.

—

And I know that what is popularly called politics is only a tiny part of what causes history to move.

—W.H. Auden[22]

In the fall of 2002, I was living in Italy. There was a growing fear that America was going to wage war in Iraq. There was also a growing resistance throughout Europe to the militant Bush-Blair partnership. An estimated one million people gathered in Florence; they walked the streets of Firenze, creating a body politic seven kilometers long.

This news was not being reported in America.

I wrote a letter home in the form of an op-ed piece for the *Salt Lake Tribune*. I wanted my community to know about this calm manifestation of willful resolve demonstrating a simple fact: Even if our political leaders cannot read the pulse of a changing world, the people do. The European Social Forum had just held its meetings in Florence, where issues ranging from health and the environment to international trade to the possibility of a war in Iraq were discussed. It ended with this gesture of movement, much of it along the banks of the Arno River, creating a river of another sort, a river of humans engaged in a diverse dialogue of peace.

Train after train stopped and emptied itself of the working middle class. Men, women, and children from Italian towns and villages gathered to participate with citizens from all over Europe. Massimo Sottani, a former mayor of Regello whom I had met in the village where I was staying,[23] had invited me to join him with his family and friends. "It is not only our right and obligation to participate in civic life, it is in our best interest," he said as we stood outside the station waiting for more of his friends.

Lorenzo Becawtini, a businessman in Florence, joined us. "Antiglobalization is not a slogan," he said, "it is a rigorous reconfiguration of democracy that places power and creativity back into the hands of villagers and townspeople, providing them with as many choices as possible."

With antiglobalization in Europe often tied to anti-Americanism, there were the inevitable placards of George W. Bush disguised as Hitler next to banners that read "DROP BUSH NOT BOMBS" and a Big Mac being driven on top of a hearse. But for the most part, the focal point of this massive demonstration remained on positive changes for a changing world.

At one point, an elderly Florentine man who held memories of Mussolini stepped out on his balcony above the wave of people and draped a white bedsheet over the railing in support of peace. As participants waved to the old man, the crowd spontaneously began singing "Ciao, Bella, Ciao," the song of the *partigianos*, the Italian resistance against the fascists in World War II. Neighbor after neighbor repeated the gesture, draping white sheets and pillow cases over their balconies until the apartment walls that lined the streets appeared as great sails billowing in the breeze.

Albertina Pisano, a twenty-five-year-old student from the University of Milan, said, "My generation in Europe doesn't know what it means to be at war. I came to the forum to listen and participate." When I asked her if she thought this would make any difference, she answered, "It is making a difference to me."

Looking over my shoulder from the rise on the bridge, all I could see was an endless river of people walking, many hand in hand, all side by side, peacefully, united in place with a will for social change.

Michelangelo was among them, as art students from Florence raised replicas of his *Prigioni* above their heads, the unfinished sculptures of prisoners trying to break free from the confines of stone.

Machiavelli was among them, as philosophy students from Rome carried his words: "There is nothing more difficult to take in hand, more perilous to conduct, or more uncertain in its success than to take the lead in the introduction of a new order of things."

Leonardo da Vinci was among them, his words carrying a particularly contemporary sting: "And by reason of their boundless pride…there shall be nothing remaining on the earth or under the earth or in the waters that shall not be pursued and molested or destroyed."

The hundreds of thousands of individuals who walked together in the name of social change could be seen as the dignified, radical center walking boldly toward the future. As an American in Florence, I wondered, how do we walk with the rest of the world when our foreign policies seem to run counter to the rising global awareness of a world hungry for honest diplomacy?

—

When I returned home to Castle Valley I went for a long walk on the sage flats. "One does not walk for peace," I recalled Thich Nhat Hahn saying. "One walks in peace."[24]

———

As I look back over the story we have been living in Castle Valley, it does not begin to convey the power and empowering nature of the process. It is through the process of defining what we want as a town that we are becoming a real community. It is through the act of participation that we change.

This is not simply a story of not-in-my-backyard. It is the unfolding tale of how a small community in the desert is rising to its own defense, saying, we believe we have a stake in the future of our own community, which we choose to define beyond our own boundaries of time and space and species.

A crisis woke us up. A shared love of place opened a dialogue with neighbors. We asked for help. We found partners. We used our collective intelligence to formulate a plan. And then we had to search within ourselves to find what each of us had to give.

In my private moments of despair, I am aware of the limits of my own imagination. I am learning in Castle Valley that imaginations shared invite collaboration and collaboration creates community. A life in association, not a life independent, is the democratic ideal. We participate in the vitality of the struggle.

This has not been easy for a town of self-defined renegades and recluses. Disagreement behind closed doors has been common. There have been times when Brooke and I have had heated discussions within our own home. I would feel he was giving away too much to SITLA in the planning process by entertaining areas of high-density housing. He thought I was being my usual recalcitrant self in only wanting to discuss open space options.

We are all having to move beyond what is comfortable. Patience is stretched. Personalities get in the way. Egos provide points of obstructions. It is never easy. We are learning to listen. We are learning to forgive. We are learning to go forward, believing what binds us together as a community is stronger than individual bickering points. And we are having a great time. Monthly potlucks are held at the Mormon church where everyone is invited, and last fall we had the first annual tractor parade during the Gourd Festival, complete with a Gourd Queen in her gilded gourd-cup brassiere riding on top of a decorated John Deere.

Beneath all this, there is an overarching faith that we will be able to keep these open lands intact, as a vital part of the integrity of Castle Valley. Faith, stamina, and trust; this we have. We trust—and trust is imperative— that we can create an economically viable and ecologically sustainable plan for the town, the land, and its creatures, alongside the interests of the Utah School

Institutional Trust Lands Administration.

Social change takes time. Communities are built on the practice of patience and imagination—the belief that we are here for the duration and will take care of our relations in times of both drought and abundance. These are the blood and flesh gestures of commitment.

Pete Seeger says, "The world is going to be saved by people saving their own homes." I believe him.

Castle Valley is one example in thousands of local narratives being written around America. Enlivened citizenship is activated each time we knock on our neighbors' doors, each time we sit down together and share a meal.

This is a town in the heart of rural Utah that believes we can begin to live differently, that the preservation of one's homeland is the preservation of the planet.

—

In our increasingly fundamentalist country, we have to remember what is fundamental: gravity—what draws us to a place and keeps us there, like love, like kinship. When we commit to a particular place, a certain element of choice is removed. We are free to dig in, and allow ourselves to be mentored by the life around us. We begin to see the world whole instead of fractured. Long-term strategies replace short-term gains. Routine opens the door to creativity. We express ourselves. We inform one another and become an educated public that responds.

Here in the redrock desert, which now carries the weight of more leases for oil and gas than its fragile red skin can support due to the aggressive energy policy of the Bush administration, the open space of democracy appears to be closing. The Rocky Mountain states are feeling this same press of energy extraction with scant thought being given to energy alternatives. A domestic imperialism has crept into our country with the same assured arrogance and ideology-of-might that seem evident in Iraq.

It is easy to believe we the people have no say, that the powers in Washington will roll over our local, on-the-ground concerns with their corporate energy ties and thumper trucks. It is easy to believe that the American will is only focused on how to get rich, how to be entertained, and how to distract itself from the hard choices we have before us as a nation.

I refuse to believe this. The only space I see truly capable of being closed is not the land or our civil liberties but our own hearts.

The human heart is the first home of democracy. It is where we embrace our questions. Can we be equitable? Can we be generous? Can we listen with our whole beings, not just our minds, and offer our attention rather than our opinions? And do we have enough resolve in our hearts to act courageously, relentlessly, without giving up—ever—trusting our fellow citizens to join with us in our determined pursuit of a living democracy?

The heart is the house of empathy whose door opens when we receive the pain of others. This is where bravery lives, where we find our mettle to give and receive, to love and be loved, to stand in the center of uncertainty with strength, not fear, understanding this is all there is. The heart is the path to wisdom because it dares to be vulnerable in the presence of power. Our power lies in our love of our homelands.

The heart embodies faith because it leads us to charity. It is the muscle behind hope that brings confidence to those who despair.

Consider this: The poet Walt Whitman waits for his president each morning, as Mr. Lincoln rides his horse to the White House, flanked by military escorts. The president passes by the white-bearded fellow who stands affectionately in Lafayette Square every day to pay his respects. The two tip hats and exchange bows, a poet and a president broken open by war.

> *Over the carnage rose prophetic a voice,*
> *Be not dishearten'd, affection shall solve the problems of*
> *freedom yet,*
> *Those who love each other shall become invincible.*[25]

Whitman cared for the wounded soldiers returning from the battlefields. Lincoln cared for a wounded nation threatened to be torn apart by slavery. Both men were purveyors of a spiritual democracy borne out of love and loss. Both men articulated the wisdom of their hearts borne out of direct engagement, one in *Leaves of Grass*, the other in the Gettysburg Address. No one told Walt Whitman how the earth tasted.

> *It is for my mouth forever, I am in love with it,*
> *I will go to the bank by the wood, and become undisguised*
> > *and naked,*
> *I am mad for it to be in contact with me.*[26]

And no one told Lincoln what grief looked like on the field of Gettysburg. He went and saw it for himself and became a compassionate witness to the Civil War.

> *We can not dedicate—we can not consecrate—we can not hallow—this ground. The brave men, living and dead, who struggled here, have consecrated it, far above our poor power to add or detract.*[27]

Democracy depends on engagement, a firsthand accounting of what one sees, what one feels, and what one thinks, followed by the artful practice of expressing the truth of our times through our own talents, gifts, and vocations.

Question. Stand. Speak. Act.

We have a history of bravery in this nation and we must call it forward now. Our future is guaranteed only by the degree of our personal involvement and commitment to an inclusive justice.

In the open space of democracy, we engage the qualities of inquiry, intuition, and love as we become a dynamic citizenry, unafraid to exercise our shared knowledge and power. We can dissent. We can vote. We can step forward in times of terror with a confounding calm that will shatter fear and complacency.

It is time to ask, when will our national culture of self-interest stop cutting the bonds of community to shore up individual gain and instead begin to nourish communal life through acts of giving, not taking? It is time to acknowledge the violence rendered to our souls each time a mountaintop is removed to expose a coal vein in Appalachia or when a wetland is drained, dredged, and filled for a strip mall. And the time has come to demand an end to the wholesale dismissal of the sacredness of life in all its variety and forms, as we witness the repeated breaking of laws, the relaxing of laws in the sole name of growth and greed.

A wild salmon is not the same as a salmon raised in a hatchery. And a prairie dog colony is not a shooting gallery for rifle recreationists, but a culture that has evolved with the prairie since the Pleistocene. At what point do we finally lay our bodies down to say this blatant disregard for biology and wild lives is no longer acceptable?

We have made the mistake of confusing democracy with capitalism and have mistaken political engagement with a political machinery we all understand to be corrupt. It is time to resist the simplistic, utilitarian view that what is good for business is good for humanity in all its complex web of relationships. A spiritual democracy is inspired by our own sense of what we can accomplish together, honoring an integrated society where the social, intellectual, physical, and economic well-being of all is considered, not just the wealth and health of the corporate few.

"A patriot must always be ready to defend his country against his government," said Edward Abbey.[28]

To not be engaged in the democratic process, to sit back and let others do the work for us, is to fall prey to bitterness and cynicism. It is the passivity of cynicism that has broken the back of our collective outrage. We succumb to our own depression believing there is nothing we can do.

John Dewey in 1937 said, "Unless democratic habits of thought and action are part of the fiber of a people, political democracy is insecure. It cannot stand in isolation. It must be buttressed by the presence of democratic methods in all social relationships."

If we cannot begin to embrace democracy as a way of life: the right to be educated, to think, discuss, dissent, create, and act, acting in imaginative and revolutionary ways...if we fail to see the necessity for each of us to participate in the formation of an ethical life...if we cannot bring a sense of equity and respect into our homes, our marriages, our schools, and our churches, alongside our local, state, and federal governments, then democracy simply becomes, as Dewey suggests, "a form of idolatry," as we descend into the basement of nationalism.

I do not believe we can look for leadership beyond ourselves. I do not believe we can wait for someone or something to save us from our global predicaments and obligations. I need to look in the mirror and ask this of myself: If I am committed to seeing the direction of our country change, how must I change myself?

We are a people addicted to speed and superficiality, a nation that prides itself on moral superiority. But our folly lies in not seeing what we base our superiority on. Wealth and freedom? What is wealth if we cannot share it? What is freedom if we cannot offer it as a vision of compassion and restraint, rather than force and aggression? Without a deepening of our thought processes as to what constitutes a living democracy, without an acknowledgment of complexity in a society of sound bites, we will not find the true source of our anger or an authentic passion that will propel us forward to the place of personal engagement. Perhaps this is what we have been longing for all along—to wrap ourselves in life.

We are in need of a reflective activism born out of humility, not arrogance. Reflection, with deep time spent in the consideration of others, opens the door to becoming a compassionate participant in the world.

"To care is neither conservative nor radical," writes John Ralston Saul. "It is a form of consciousness."[29]

Are we ready for the next evolutionary leap—to recognize the restoration of democracy as the restoration of liberty and justice for all species, not just our own? To be in the service of something beyond ourselves—to be in the presence of something other than ourselves, together—this is where we can begin to craft a meaningful life where personal isolation and despair disappear through the shared engagement of a vibrant citizenry.

—

Summer 2004: Parriott Mesa—a freefall of fire—politically incorrect but spiritually compelling. It is the Seventh Day of Adventists high school graduation and this is their yearly ritual of commencement. All the valley waits and watches with great anticipation. The school resides in Castle Valley. The students farm the land alongside their lessons. Each year, graduates hike the steep walls of the mesa and ignite a huge bonfire on top. From the valley floor, it appears as a star resting on the bow of a massive ship of slickrock. When the fire grows to its maximum height, the students push it off the ledge. We watch a freefall of flames. It is not water. But fire.

This is what our community is in need of now. Fire. Fire that wakes us up. Fire that transforms where we are. Fire to see our way through the dark. Fire as illumination. We witness from the front porches of our homes the exhilaration of pushing an idea over the edge until it ignites a community, and we can never look at Parriott Mesa again without remembering the way it was sold,

the way a sign disappeared and reappeared in Arches
National Park, the way the community bought the land
back through the gift of anonymity, and the breathing
space it now holds as the red rock cornerstone of Castle
Valley.

On this magical night, we watch in wonder and awe as
young people climb, carrying wood on their backs, and
lay down their burdens, striking the match, blowing on
embers, fanning the flames with great faith and joy. Fire.
Fire in a freefall, over the cliff, reminding us all what is
primal and fleeting. We cannot know what lies ahead. We
may be unsure how to bring our prayers forward. But on
this night in the desert, we celebrate this cascading river
of beauty.

Notes

Commencement

1.

Hope is the thing with feathers
That perches in the soul,
And sings the tune without the words
And never stops at all,

And sweetest in the gale is heard;
And sore must be the storm
That could abash the little bird
That kept so many warm.

I've heard it in the chillest land,
And on the strangest sea;
Yet, never, in extremity,
It asked a crumb of me.

—Emily Dickinson

2. Lincoln-Douglas debates, September 11, 1858,
Edwardsville, Illinois. *The Collected Works of Abraham
Lincoln*, edited by Roy P. Basler. New Brunswick:
Rutgers University Press, 1990.

3. "Malo periculosam libertatem quam quietam servitutem." Thomas Jefferson to James Madison, Jan. 30, 1787. *The Republic of Letters: The Correspondence Between Thomas Jefferson and James Madison, 1776–1826*, edited by James M. Smith. New York: Norton, 1995, v. 1: p. 461.

4. Henry David Thoreau, *Walden and Civil Disobedience: Or, Life in the Woods*. New York: Signet Classics, 1999, with an introduction by W. S. Merwin, p. 276.

5. On March 8, 2003, twenty-three women were arrested for "stationary demonstration" in front of The White House during a Code Pink antiwar march and held inside the Anacostia Correctional Unit (D.C. Jail) in locked cells for several hours without the aid of an attorney.

Here are their names: Rev. Patricia Ackerman, Krystal Akens, Deborah Alves, Rachel Bagby, Medea Benjamin, Brianna Binkerd-Dale, Bean Finneky, Amy Goodman, Marian Greene, Susan Griffin, Maxine Hong Kingston, Marian McWhorter, Kirsten Michael, Jessica Miller, Marian Moore, Gael Murphy, Emily Nella, Carol Ann Nelson, Bonnie Rubenstein, Holly Shere, Helen Taylor, Donna Kaye Tharpe, Alice Walker, Terry Tempest Williams, Karen Wisniewski, Nina Utne.

For more details, see "With Passion and a Dash of Pink, Women Gather to Protest," *The New York Times*, March 9, 2003.

6. See Sheryl Gay Stolberg's article, "Washington Talk:

Some Wholly New Work for Old Washington Hand,"
The New York Times, October 22, 2003.

*He said he was giving a speech at the University of Utah in
May when he remarked that he "would serve this country
whenever called." When he got back to his hotel, he said, the
office of the defense secretary, Donald H. Rumsfeld, telephoned,
asking him to go to Baghdad. Then Bremer called. "I said,
'Did you guys hear my speech?'" Korologos recalled.*

7. Umberto Eco and Cardinal Martini, *Belief or
Nonbelief? A Confrontation*. New York: Arcade Publishing,
1997 (English translation 2000), p. 71.

8. "Freedom of Speech." In *Poets Against the War*, edited
by Sam Hamill. New York: Thunder's Mouth
Press/Nation Books, 2003, p. 227.

9. William Faulkner, *Essays, Speeches, and Public Letters*.
New York: Random House, 1965.

10. "Neither Victims or Executioners." In *The Power of
Nonviolence: Writings by Advocates of Peace*. Boston: Beacon
Press, 2002, p. 72.

11. Ibid, p. 73.

Ground Truthing

12. Adolph Murie, *A Naturalist in Alaska*. Tucson: University of Arizona Press, reprint edition, 1990.

13. Norman Hallendy, *Inuksuit: Silent Messengers of the Arctic*. Seattle: University of Washington Press, 2001.

14. Subhankar Banerjee, *Arctic National Wildlife Refuge: Seasons of Life and Land*. Seattle: Mountaineers Books, 2003.

15. Not long after Cindy Shogan and I had returned home from the Canning River, we paid Senator Durbin a visit in his office in Washington, D.C. He, too, had just returned from camping in the Arctic National Wildlife Refuge with his son during the August congressional recess. He said how important it was for him to have seen the refuge personally so he can speak on the Senate floor with firsthand knowledge. In his enthusiasm, he shared with us his written impressions. This is an excerpt:

President Bush believes that America's energy appetite is so compelling that we must abandon a fifty-year commitment to preserve this untouched corner of our nation. In 1960, President Eisenhower established the ANWR, declaring this area an important national treasure to be protected in perpetuity. But President Bush has proposed several decades of development and drilling in the Arctic National Wildlife Refuge to deliver a six-month supply of our nation's energy needs.

Standing on the banks of the Canning River one wonders whether our super-size, use-it-and-toss-it generation is not displaying a shortsightedness and selfishness that is a sad lesson for our children.

An amendment I offered to the Energy bill would have required automakers to build more fuel-efficient cars over the next ten years. According to the National Academy of Sciences, cars averaging 40 miles per gallon are attainable with current technology. My amendment for fuel-efficient vehicles would have saved over 10 times the amount of oil we could glean from ANWR.

The amendment was opposed by the White House, the oil companies, automakers, and their unions. The final vote fell short by a 32–64 margin.

The voices for conservation and responsible environmental stewardship were drowned out by the roar of special interests groups on Capitol Hill.

16. John Kauffman, *Brooks Range*. Seattle: Mountaineers Books, 1992.

17. Olaus Murie's statement was submitted to U.S. Congress. Senate. Committee on Interstate and Foreign Commerce. Subcommittee on Merchant Marine and Fisheries. Hearings, S.1889, *A Bill to Authorize the Establishment of the Arctic Wildlife Range, Alaska*, 86th Cong., 1st sess., part 1, 30 June 1959 (Washington, D.C.: GPO, 1960), p. 58–59.

18. When we smelled those wild sweet peas wafting on the wind, I thought about Anna Pavord, a British writer of extraordinary skill and sensitivity. She is the author of *The Tulip*. When we were in Italy together at a writers' retreat, we were talking about the healing capacity of nature. I shared with her my mother's story of her illness with ovarian cancer, how she was held in the healing grace of the land. Anna told me her own story. Shortly after being operated on for stomach cancer, she was in extreme pain, but did not like what the morphine was doing to her mind, how it made her feel. She wanted to be taken off the morphine drip. The doctor said she would not be able to endure the pain. She asked her husband and daughters to make nosegays of sweet peas from her garden in the country and bring them to her in the hospital. Instead of morphine, she made a mask of sweet peas for herself and breathed their sweet fragrance deep into her lungs. What she knew was this: Sweet peas have similar medicinal properties like morphine and can curb pain through the potency of their aroma. Anna's pain was eased.

19. "Democratic Vistas." In *The Portable Walt Whitman*. New York: Viking Press, 1945, p. 448. (I love this older edition I found in the Lippincott Bookstore in Bangor, Maine, with an introduction and critical commentary by Mark Van Doren.)

20. Ibid, p. 423.

Engagement

21. On January 15, 1998, President Bill Clinton also gave the Medal of Freedom Award to Arnold Aronson, Brooke Astor, Robert Coles, Justin Dart, Jr., James Farmer, Frances Hesselbein, Fred Korematsu, Sol Linowitz, Wilma Mankiller, Mario G. Obledo, Elliot L. Richardson, David Rockefeller, Albert Shanker, and Elmo Russell ("Bud") Zumwalt, Jr.

22. W. H. Auden, *The Prolific and the Devourer.* Hopewell, NJ: Ecco Press, reprint edition, 1996, p. 98. In this provocative essay on the relationship between the artist and the politician written in 1939, Auden writes, "The greater part of your political effect…does not come from the specifically political work you do but from your everyday working and private life, the hours you spend teaching, the money you spend in shops, buses, cinemas, etc. What is required of an individual is that he shall try always to increase his knowledge of how to act effectively and try always not to act contrary to his knowledge. Only in that way is it possible to raise the average level of the masses and so to improve political action."

23. *A week before the manifestation in Florence, I attended a dinner at Sandro Bennini's home where I had the good fortune of meeting Massimo Sottani. I wrote this account of the evening that I wanted to share with readers because I believe it speaks to the power of personal engagement and how we can partici-*

pate in the open space of democracy, each in our own way, each with our own gifts.

We knocked on the large wooden door and waited. Sandro Bennini, the baker in the village of Donnini, had invited us to dinner. Four of us staying at a friend's home just down the road, accepted.

Sandro opened the door and with a wide, sweeping gesture of his hand welcomed us inside. He was dressed in tails, a full black tuxedo with a gardenia over his heart.

In an instant, we could see that all furniture had been moved out of the living room and replaced with an enormous square table lavishly set for forty people, ten on each side. Two, three-tier bronze candelabra were lit casting shadows on a centerpiece of stuffed roosters, grapes, olives, figs, pomegranates and mushrooms, all familiar to a Tuscan household.

At each place setting of bone china, silver, and crystal goblets, there was a parchment scroll with burned edges tied neatly with a white satin ribbon. Once opened, it proclaimed the six-course menu to come: *Deep-fried seasonal vegetables; cream of pumpkin soup; tiny squash-filled crepes; Lesso ritatto (Tuscan specialty); roast of wild boar with herbs; gelato; and biscotti with espresso.*

The house filled with guests, stunned by the elaborate celebration. Like us, most had anticipated a casual gathering. None of us were appropriately dressed. Our postures corrected what our clothes could not.

"Welcome, my friends," Sandro said. "I invite you to

sit down at this Table of Peace. With the heart, anything is possible." He smiled and then said, "Tonight, I share with you my gifts of bread and song." And then with both hands extended the width of the table, he said with great gusto, "*Godere*. Enjoy."

Chianti was poured, toasts were made with glasses raised high. A pianist emerged as waiters appeared with the first bowls of soup. Suddenly, Sandro the Baker became Sandro the Tenor and so began this evening in Tuscany where we were invited to a feast of Italian arias that lasted well into the next day.

In that candlelit night of magic, Sandro Bennini held back nothing. He sang for hours, offering us his passion for food and music, his gifts of drama and decorum, and shared them relentlessly with his eyes closed and his hands over his heart.

As the evening progressed with each entrée more elaborate than the next, all created from foods from the region be it handmade pasta, wild boar, or roasted chestnuts, the pitch of love continued to rise like a great crescendo.

The village priest sang songs of lost Florentine virgins alongside Sandro. An Italian named Marco stood on top of his chair and blew kisses to all saying this was a night to remember that all bad love affairs eventually turn good through the memory of time. And wine. A German tourist who had visited Sandro's bakery earlier that day fell asleep and was snoring in time with the music, rising and falling with each bel canto. The former mayor of Regello, Massimo Sottani, was sitting next to me. He whispered the story of a gold-leaf triptych painted by Masaccio that has hung in his village's church since 1421. He spoke about how the eyes of the painting had presided over births and deaths and daily masses, that the Uffizi Gallery begged for it to be housed in Florence but the people of Cascia said no. The triptych belonged to the village.

And across the table, I could see other enchantments turning in all directions through private conversations as cats foraged beneath the dinner table, their tails tickling our legs as Sandro continued to sing with his eyes closed. In that moment, it became clear that the great Italian filmmaker Fellini was simply a documentarian.

What I learned in Italy is that beauty is not optional. It resides at the core of each conversation, around each dinner table. Beauty nourishes our soul alongside food. It allows us to remember not only what is possible, what we are capable of creating as human beings, but what is necessary. Each of us bears gifts and we can share them within the embrace of our own communities, even around the Table of Peace.

We, Americans of puritanical origins, have much to learn. Why do we hold back both our gifts and our passions in the name of what is proper? Modesty in its extreme is nothing more than clothed repression, in the end, covering what we all know is there—our longing to share our inward and outward beauty. How can there be shame in this desire to expose the best of who we are? If we choose to hide or minimize our gifts, how can we ever embrace hope?

In times of war, it seems to me the only appropriate action is to bare our hearts fearlessly with love and generosity, sharing the gifts that we have been given, whatever they may be, freely with those around us.

Sandro Bennini, through his gifts of bread and song, baked and sung world peace heroically around his own dinner table. It didn't matter if the meal was served on time, though it was. It didn't matter if he sometimes sang off key, which he did. What mattered was the beauty of his intention, to bring people together in his village who had never met before and in so doing, celebrated the exuberant, joyous, tender unpredictability of humanity. In the sanctuary of his home, anything was possible, because all hearts were open.

(This story was written just prior to the Iraq war and appeared in *Hope* magazine, Spring 2003).

24. On September 10 and 11, 2003, I made a pilgrimage to Washington, D.C. I wanted to return to where I had been on September 11, 2001, and make peace with the terror that had lodged inside my bones.

Thich Nhat Hahn, the Zen Buddhist monk from Vietnam, had been invited to address members of Congress, their staffs, and their families in the Library of Congress on the eve of this anniversary. If there were extra seats, the public was welcome. His talk "Leading with Courage and Compassion," was sponsored by The

Faith & Politics Institute, an organization made up of members of Congress that provides occasions for moral reflection and spiritual community to political leaders, drawing wisdom from a range of religious traditions. The Institute encourages civility and respect as spiritual values essential to democracy.

Cindy Shogan and I attended the lecture together.

Congresswoman Lois Capps from California introduced Thich Nhat Hahn. She spoke about the need in Washington for a different kind of leadership. She quoted Thomas Merton:

It is true, political problems are not solved by love and mercy, but the world of politics is not the only world, and unless political decisions rest on a foundation of something better and higher than politics, they can never do any real good for humanity.... There must be a new force, the power of love, the power of understanding and human compassion, the strength of selflessness and cooperation, and the creative dynamism of the will to live and to build and the will to forgive...the will for reconciliation.

She reminded the audience that the Reverend Martin Luther King, Jr. had nominated Thich Nhat Hahn for the Nobel Peace Prize for his spiritual resistance during the Vietnam War. She spoke of her gratitude that he would make this special visit to honor the anniversary of September 11 and share his insights of how we might govern this country in a way that promotes peace instead of repeating the tyranny of violence.

Congresswoman Capps then held a moment of silence before she turned the time over to Thich Nhat Hahn.

Thich Nhat Hahn entered the stage of the Library of Congress quietly dressed in his brown robes. He sat on a cushion on the floor. The silence already created was extended and filled the audience like a prayer.

He then began to speak. "In Congress, in city halls, in statehouses, and schools, we need people capable of practicing deep listening and loving speech. Unfortunately, many of us have lost this capacity. To have peace, we must first have understanding, and understanding is not possible without gentle, loving communication. Therefore, restoring communication is an essential practice for peace."

Bells rang. At first, I thought these were Buddhist bells, but then a dozen or more members of Congress rose from their seats and left the auditorium. A vote was on the floor. A few members stayed.

Thich Nhat Hahn never broke from his line of thought, "Even if one of you practices deep listening, the tone of Congress will shift." He looked into the audience. "Even if we can prevail and listen for only one hour, the other person will obtain a great deal of relief. Listening with an open heart, we are able to keep compassion alive. Then we give the other person a real chance to express his or her feelings."

It was stunning to contemplate: members of United States Congress actually listening to one another. Members of our own communities hearing what another person with an opposing view has to say.

When the lecture was over, he invited questions.

"How are we to proceed with compassion when we watch our government's violent policies ravage the environment: the rivers, the forests, the deserts? What is appropriate action alongside contemplation," I asked, aware that my voice was shaking.

Thich Nhat Hahn spoke of the problem of consumption, the need to live more simply, that our extravagant lifestyle in America is its own form of violence on the planet.

"Dear friends, please take care of yourself if you want to protect the environment. The very well-being of the planet depends on the way you handle your body, your feelings, your perceptions, and your consciousness....If you cannot deal with the problem of consumption, and the problem of pollution and violence within you, how can you deal with problems of consumption and pollution and violence outside of you in nature?"

We listened to his last words: "When we allow ourselves the time to look deeply, we give understanding and compassion a chance to grow in our hearts, and we can then act on our insights."

Cindy and I left with more questions than answers and the burden of "leading with courage and compassion" not resting in the laps of lawmakers, but in our own. I recognized Congressman Tom Udall from New Mexico. He and his staff were talking with one another and then we watched him leave the Library of Congress alone with his head bowed.

25. Walt Whitman, "Over the Carnage Rose Prophetic A Voice," lines 1–4, *Leaves of Grass.* Brooklyn, New York: Rome Brothers, 1855.

26. Walt Whitman, "Song of Myself," Section 1, lines 14–17, *Leaves of Grass.*

27. Abraham Lincoln, The Gettysburg Address, delivered on November 19, 1863.

28. Edward Abbey, *A Cry in the Wilderness.* New York: St. Martin's Press, 1991, p. 17.

29. John Ralston Saul, *On Equilibrium.* New York: Four Walls Eight Windows, 2004, p. 45.

The will of beauty will propel us forward.

Acknowledgments

The Orion Society embodies a democratic vision of open communion, especially surrounding issues of landscape and culture and the politics that threatens both. Marion Gilliam and Laurie Lane-Zucker have been remarkable in their support of this work and the aesthetics involved. I want to thank them for their faith and wisdom in helping me to formulate these ideas of an open space of democracy.

Jennifer Sahn has been my editor for this triptych of essays that appeared first in *Orion* magazine. Rarely does one have the privilege to work with an editor as wise as she is, and as meticulous with each word. I have loved this collaboration between women.

Patrick Kelly introduced me to the Faith and Politics Institute in Washington, D.C., and I have appreciated our discussions on the balance between contemplation and action. His work on the creation of this book has been pivotal in bringing all the details together.

The entire staff of the Orion Society, especially Jason Houston, Peter Stiglin, Erik Hoffner, David Whitman, Karen Gagne, and Hal Clifford, has been an extraordinary example of what a community of friends can accomplish together.

Mary Frank continues to remind me why the arts matter to a free society. Just before the Iraq war in January 2003, she drew an image of a figure speaking, the human voice creating a bridge in a gesture she calls "Utterance." It was this image that fueled these essays. I am indebted to her for the generous companionship of her art and for the organic power of her creative and political engagement.

Brooke and my traveling companions on the Canning River created the heart of "Ground Truthing." Our love to Carol Kasza, Jim McDonald, Kyle McDonald, all of Arctic Treks; Cindy Shogan for her brilliant optimism behind the Alaska Wilderness League; Brooks Yeager, Abby Thomas, Amy Campion, and most especially, Tom Campion, for his generosity of spirit and whose love of the Arctic National Wildlife Refuge has fueled a generation of activists and impassioned political leaders.

Early on, Steven Rockefeller suggested I go back into the work of John Dewey and this has made an extraordinary difference. "Democracy is not an alternative to other principles of associated life. It is the idea of community life itself."

The following people have also been important in the formulation of these essays: J. D. Williams, Robert Newman, Bernie Machen, Senator Robert F. Bennett, Senator Richard Durbin, Representative Jim McDermott, Representative Marcy Kaptur, Sam Hamill, William Merwin, Peter Lewis, Emily Warn, Professor Wangari Maathai, Rita and John Elder, Jan Sloan, Mary O'Brien, Ginny Wood, Roger Kay, Debbie Miller, Subhankar Banerjee, Inger Koetz, Florence Krall Shephard, Nancy Shea, Lyn Dalebout, Lynne Tempest, Ann and Steve Tempest, Audrey Rust, Kathyrn Morelli, Antje and Paul Newhagen, Liz Thomas, Carolyn Cleveland, Kim Ripley, Monette Clark, Jack Campbell and the Moab Peace Group, Beatrice Monti della Corte, Anna Pavord, Tomáz Salamun, Diran Adebayo, Massimo Sottani, Maxine Hong Kingston, Susan Griffin, Alice Walker, Nina Utne, Nancy Caulfield, Medea Benjamin, Gael Murphy, Michelle Shocked, and Rachel Bagby.

The students at Kalamazoo Community College and Evergreen College were instrumental in my critical thinking about political engagement.

Nick Sichterman and Mariah Hughs of Blue Hill Books in Maine, Betsy Burton of The King's English, and José Knighton of Back of Beyond Books in Utah, have been generous in discussing these ideas before publication.

My deepest gratitude belongs to the Castle Rock Collaboration and the community of Castle Valley for their neighborly support, creativity, and courage in creating conversation and the quiet movement toward social change as neighbors.

My father, John Tempest, keeps me honest, reminding me in no uncertain terms, we do not all think the same. On numerous occasions, Brooke and I walked into his guest room in Salt Lake City to spend the night, only to find a photograph of Laura and George W. Bush propped against the pillows welcoming us home.

Carl Brandt has my enduring devotion for his integrity and care.

And as always, my love to Brooke for the open space of democracy that resides within our own home.

Publisher's Acknowledgments

The Orion Society would like to thank Tom Campion and Charla Brown and the Ruth Brown Foundation for their generous support of this book. We would also like to thank the many hundreds of individual citizens and foundations that have supported The Orion Society's Thoughts on America Initiative, of which this project is a part, including Priscilla Lewis and her colleagues at the Rockefeller Brothers Fund, Deborah Reich, Scott and Ruth Sanders, Terry Marbach and the Namaste Foundation, Peter Barnes, Debbi Brainerd, Phillip and Julie Gardner, and Peter Schuyler.

About the Author

Terry Tempest Williams lives in Castle Valley, Utah. Her books include *Refuge: An Unnatural History of Family and Place*; *An Unspoken Hunger*; *Desert Quartet*; *Leap*; and *Red: Passion and Patience in the Desert*. She is the recipient of a John Simon Guggenheim Fellowship and a Lannan Literary Fellowship in creative nonfiction. Her work has appeared in *The New Yorker*, *The Nation*, *The New York Times*, *Orion*, *Parabola*, and *The Best American Essays*. She is currently the Annie Clark Tanner Scholar in Environmental Humanities at the University of Utah.

About Mary Frank

Mary Frank is an American artist known for the organic strength of both her sculpture and painting. Her work has been widely exhibited and is held in many public collections, including the Metropolitan Museum of Art in New York, the Art Institute of Chicago, and the Museum of Fine Arts in Boston.

Desert Quartet: An Erotic Landscape (Pantheon, 1995) was her first collaboration with Terry Tempest Williams. She has collaborated with Peter Matthiessen on *Shadows of Africa* (Abrams, 1992), a collection of words and images conveying the animals in the African wild.

An environmental and social activist, Mary Frank is deeply committed to the work of Solar Cookers International and has created political posters in support of human rights around the world. Her large-scale puppets and placards have been central to many antiwar demonstrations.

Mary Frank has received two Guggenheim fellowships and was elected to the American Academy and Institute of Arts and Letters in 1984. She is married to the renowned musicologist Leo Treitler. Her art is represented by the D.C. Moore Gallery in New York.

The Orion Society

The Orion Society's mission is to inform, inspire, and engage individuals and grassroots organizations in becoming a significant cultural force for healing nature and community. For more information on The Orion Society's publications and programs, please visit www.OrionOnline.org.